READINGS ON

# CHARLES DICKENS

## Other titles in the Greenhaven Press Literary Companion Series:

**AMERICAN AUTHORS**

Maya Angelou
Stephen Crane
Emily Dickinson
William Faulkner
F. Scott Fitzgerald
Nathaniel Hawthorne
Ernest Hemingway
Herman Melville
Arthur Miller
Eugene O'Neill
Edgar Allan Poe
John Steinbeck
Mark Twain

**BRITISH AUTHORS**

Jane Austen
Joseph Conrad

**WORLD AUTHORS**

Fyodor Dostoyevsky
Homer
Sophocles

**AMERICAN LITERATURE**

The Great Gatsby
Of Mice and Men
The Scarlet Letter

**BRITISH LITERATURE**

Animal Farm
The Canterbury Tales
Lord of the Flies
Romeo and Juliet
Shakespeare: The Comedies
Shakespeare: The Sonnets
Shakespeare: The Tragedies
A Tale of Two Cities

**WORLD LITERATURE**

Diary of a Young Girl

THE GREENHAVEN PRESS

*Literary Companion*

TO BRITISH AUTHORS

READINGS ON

# CHARLES DICKENS

David Bender, *Publisher*

Bruno Leone, *Executive Editor*

Brenda Stalcup, *Managing Editor*

Bonnie Szumski, *Series Editor*

Clarice Swisher, *Book Editor*

Greenhaven Press, San Diego, CA

Every effort has been made to trace the owners of copyrighted material. The articles in this volume may have been edited for content, length, and/or reading level. The titles have been changed to enhance the editorial purpose of the Opposing Viewpoints® concept. Those interested in locating the original source will find the complete citation on the first page of each article.

Library of Congress Cataloging-in-Publication Data

Charles Dickens / Clarice Swisher, book editor.
    p.     cm. — (The Greenhaven Press literary companion to British authors)
    Includes bibliographical references and index.
    ISBN 1-56510-590-7 (lib. bdg. : alk. paper). — ISBN 1-56510-589-3 (pbk. : alk. paper)
    1. Dickens, Charles, 1812–1870—Criticism and interpretation. I. Swisher, Clarice, 1933–  . II. Series.
PR4588.R36   1998
823'.8—dc21                      97-10493
                                     CIP

Cover photo: The Bettmann Archive

Copyright ©1998 by Greenhaven Press, Inc.
PO Box 289009
San Diego, CA 92198-9009
Printed in the U.S.A.

**"I am the affectionate father to every child of my fancy."**

*Charles Dickens*

# CONTENTS

## Chapter 1: Major Themes in Dickens's Novels

## Chapter 2: Entertaining Stories for Serial Publication

ters of Weller and Jingle and creates two funny episodes, or set pieces—a party and a trial.

# Chapter 3: Dickens's Semiautobiographical Novels

## Chapter 4: Novels of Reform, History, and Morality

the end, he has deftly fitted them into the major story and used them to enrich his theme.

# FOREWORD

*"'Tis the good reader that
makes the good book."*

Ralph Waldo Emerson

The story's bare facts are simple: The captain, an old and scarred seafarer, walks with a peg leg made of whale ivory. He relentlessly drives his crew to hunt the world's oceans for the great white whale that crippled him. After a long search, the ship encounters the whale and a fierce battle ensues. Finally the captain drives his harpoon into the whale, but the harpoon line catches the captain about the neck and drags him to his death.

A simple story, a straightforward plot—yet, since the 1851 publication of Herman Melville's *Moby-Dick*, readers and critics have found many meanings in the struggle between Captain Ahab and the whale. To some, the novel is a cautionary tale that depicts how Ahab's obsession with revenge leads to his insanity and death. Others believe that the whale represents the unknowable secrets of the universe and that Ahab is a tragic hero who dares to challenge fate by attempting to discover this knowledge. Perhaps Melville intended Ahab as a criticism of Americans' tendency to become involved in well-intentioned but irrational causes. Or did Melville model Ahab after himself, letting his fictional character express his anger at what he perceived as a cruel and distant god?

Although literary critics disagree over the meaning of *Moby-Dick*, readers do not need to choose one particular interpretation in order to gain an understanding of Melville's novel. Instead, by examining various analyses, they can gain numerous insights into the issues that lie under the surface of the basic plot. Studying the writings of literary critics can also aid readers in making their own assessments of *Moby-Dick* and other literary works and in developing analytical thinking skills.

The Greenhaven Literary Companion Series was created with these goals in mind. Designed for young adults, this unique anthology series provides an engaging and comprehensive introduction to literary analysis and criticism. The essays included in the Literary Companion Series are chosen for their accessibility to a young adult audience and are expertly edited in consideration of both the reading and comprehension levels of this audience. In addition, each essay is introduced by a concise summation that presents the contributing writer's main themes and insights. Every anthology in the Literary Companion Series contains a varied selection of critical essays that cover a wide time span and express diverse views. Wherever possible, primary sources are represented through excerpts from authors' notebooks, letters, and journals and through contemporary criticism.

Each title in the Literary Companion Series pays careful consideration to the historical context of the particular author or literary work. In-depth biographies and detailed chronologies reveal important aspects of authors' lives and emphasize the historical events and social milieu that influenced their writings. To facilitate further research, every anthology includes primary and secondary source bibliographies of articles and/or books selected for their suitability for young adults. These engaging features make the Greenhaven Literary Companion Series ideal for introducing students to literary analysis in the classroom or as a library resource for young adults researching the world's great authors and literature.

Exceptional in its focus on young adults, the Greenhaven Literary Companion Series strives to present literary criticism in a compelling and accessible format. Every title in the series is intended to spark readers' interest in leading American and world authors, to help them broaden their understanding of literature, and to encourage them to formulate their own analyses of the literary works that they read. It is the editors' hope that young adult readers will find these anthologies to be true companions in their study of literature.

# INTRODUCTION

How Charles Dickens told his stories and how he gave form to the cast of memorable characters that drew thousands of Victorian readers to his books is the subject of *Readings on Charles Dickens*. Most of Dickens's work was originally published in serial form; readers in his day waited for Dickens's next installment of a story. He made them laugh at Pickwick and cry when Little Nell died; he made them care about prisons and poor children and mistreated factory workers. In *Charles Dickens: The Last of the Great Men*, G.K. Chesterton states, "Whatever the word 'great' means, Dickens was what it meant." This companion provides teachers and students with a biography and a wide variety of critical opinion to help them discover the art and ideas that give Dickens his greatness. Essays have been selected to identify the major themes that exist throughout Dickens's works and to explain the particular stylistic and structural devices in major individual works.

*Readings on Charles Dickens* includes many special features that make research and literary criticism accessible and understandable. An annotated table of contents lets readers quickly preview the contents of individual essays. A chronology features a list of significant events in Dickens's life placed in a broader historical context. The bibliography includes books on Dickens's time and additional critical sources suitable for research.

Each essay has aids for clear understanding. The introductions serve as directed reading for the essays by explaining main points, which are further identified by subheads within the essays. Footnotes identify uncommon references and define unfamiliar words. An occasional insert has been included to illustrate a point made in the essay or a feature of Dickens's prose. Taken together, these aids make the Greenhaven Press Literary Companion Series an indispensable research tool.

# CHARLES DICKENS: A BIOGRAPHY

Charles Dickens exuded an energy and determination that awed friends and overwhelmed relatives. His temper flared at slights to himself and his work; his generosity and compassion extended to children and the working poor. He was a pessimist who doubted that government and the upper class would ever pass reforms to help poor people, but who optimistically believed in the goodness of the lower class and championed their cause throughout his life. He made his mark in nineteenth-century England with humor, creating a cast of characters that exemplified all that he loved and satirized all that he hated about his society. Biographer Edgar Johnson says in the preface to his biography of Dickens:

> Dickens was himself a Dickens character, bursting with an inordinate and fantastic vitality. The world in which his spirit dwelt was identical with the world of his novels, brilliant in hue, violent in movement, crammed with people all furiously alive and with places as alive as his people. "The Dickens world" was his everyday world.

Scholars attribute much of the formation of Dickens's personality and, consequently, his achievements to two phases in his boyhood years. The first, happy phase gave him hope and optimism; the second, sad phase instilled his spirit for social reform.

Charles John Huffman Dickens was born on February 7, 1812, in the southwestern English town of Landport in Portsea, the second of eight children born to John and Elizabeth Barrow Dickens. John Dickens, a clerk in the Navy Payoffice, and Elizabeth, a pretty, educated woman, belonged to the middle class, but were not prosperous enough to withstand the extravagant spending and entertainment they enjoyed. John Dickens enjoyed a house full of party guests and rehearsed little Charles and his sister to entertain them. In *Charles Dickens: A Critical Study,* G.K. Chesterton says:

> Some of the earliest glimpses we have of Charles Dickens show him to us perched on some chair or table singing comic

songs in an atmosphere of perpetual applause. So, almost as soon as he can toddle, he steps into the glare of the footlights. He never stepped out of it until he died.

In 1814 John was temporarily sent to the London office before being transferred to the naval dockyards in the southeastern town of Chatham in 1817, when Charles was five. There John rented a large house for his family, two servants, and Aunt Fanny, his wife's widowed sister, but soon found it beyond his means and moved his family to a smaller Chatham home.

## A HAPPY AND SAD CHILDHOOD

In a family that felt financially secure, Charles enjoyed his years in Chatham, five years that permanently affected his outlook on life. He played games with friends, put on magic-lantern shows (an early form of slide projector), and continued to sing duets with his sister Fanny. Mary Weller, the maid who cared for the children, told bedtime stories and hummed evensong, or evening worship, hymns. Dickens investigated the town, recording in his mind the sights of its shipwrights, convict laborers, guild hall, cathedral, and castle on the hill and the smells of rope and wood and canvas down by the docks. Because he was often sick, Charles never played sports well, but he loved to read, saying later, "When I think of it, the picture always arises in my mind of a summer evening, the boys at play in the churchyard, and I sitting on my bed, reading as if for life." In addition to reading the family books, such as *Peregrine Pickle, Don Quixote,* and *Robinson Crusoe,* Aunt Fanny's suitor, Dr. Matthew Lamert, and his son James took Charles to farces, melodramas, and to *Richard II* and *Macbeth.*

Dickens attended the school of William Giles, a Baptist minister in Chatham. A precocious child, Charles fully expected to attend both school and college and enter a profession. These early happy years laid the groundwork for his lifelong hope and vitality.

His hopes for a bright future were dashed, however, when his father, now heavily in debt, was transferred back to London in 1822, when Charles was ten. John Dickens settled his family in Camden Town, a poor section of London, in a four-room house that held Dickens's parents as well as six children, one maid, and James Lamert, who lived with them. No arrangement was made for Charles to go to school, though

Fanny had won a scholarship to the Royal Academy of Music. Charles did chores at home, and just as curiously as he had done in Chatham, he wandered the streets of Camden Town, observing its noisy vehicles, small factories, taverns, cooked-food stalls, and rubbish dumps and watching chimney sweeps, muffin-boys, and apprentices at work—all sounds, sights, and smells that imprinted themselves on his mind.

Not long after moving to London, Charles learned what it meant to be poor. One sad day his family sold his beloved books from Chatham days to pay debts, after which he borrowed copies of the newspapers *Spectator* and *Tatler* for his reading. His mother rented a room and started a school, but not one pupil came. James Lamert, who managed a bootblacking factory, suggested that Charles work there to help with the deteriorating family finances. At twelve, Charles worked from eight A.M. to eight P.M. for six shillings a week in the tumbledown warehouse tying and labeling pots of blacking. Two weeks after Charles started at the blacking factory, John Dickens was arrested for not paying his debts and sent to Marshalsea, a debtors prison, or workhouse for the poor, with meager food and hard labor. Charles was sent out to pawn household goods, and when only beds, chairs, and the kitchen table were left, the rest of the family moved to Marshalsea (which admitted groups in family quarters) with the father.

John Dickens, who still drew a small naval salary, paid for lodgings so that Charles could continue his job at the blacking factory. Now that he had to feed himself on six shillings a week, he divided his money into packages, one for each day, occasionally splurging the whole day's allotment on a sweet or a good ale; when he had no money, he walked to the Covent Garden market and stared at food. Alone in the lodging house with no companion but the boys from the blacking factory, who mocked him because he was small and shy and different, Charles suffered greatly. In an unpublished autobiography, he later wrote of this time in his life:

> No words can express the secret agony of my soul, as I sunk into this companionship; compared these everyday associates with those of my happier childhood; and felt my early hopes of growing up to be a learned and distinguished man, crushed in my breast.

> The deep remembrance of the sense I had of being utterly ne-

glected and hopeless; of the shame I felt in my position; of the
misery it was to my young heart to believe that, day by day,
what I had learned, and thought, and delighted in, and raised
my fancy and my emulation up by, was passing away from
me, never to be brought back any more; . . . even now, famous
and caressed and happy, I . . . wander desolately back to that
time of my life. . . . That I suffered in secret, and that I suffered exquisitely, no one ever knew but I.

Following a quarrel with John Dickens, Lamert fired
Charles after twenty weeks that seemed to Charles like
twenty years. The experience of the blacking factory made
an indelible impression on him, setting in him a hard determination, but through his suffering he developed an equally
permanent sensitivity from which he created in his novels a
host of suffering children and other innocent victims of injustice and pain.

After three months in Marshalsea, John Dickens's mother
died and John inherited £450, enough to get him out of
prison, and John went back to his job with the navy. From
1824 to 1826, he sent Charles to Wellington House Academy,
where Charles studied English, French, Latin, writing,
mathematics, and dancing. When John lost his job and took
work as a reporter for the *British Press,* he was again deep in
debt, and Charles had to drop out of school. He took a job at
the law office of Ellis and Blackmore, which he found so
boring that he determined never to be a lawyer who spent
his life "splitting hairs slowly and growing rich on the dis-
tress of others." Dickens then set out to educate himself. He
taught himself shorthand in eighteen months, went to acting
school, and procured a pass to the Reading Room in the
British Museum (the national library) where he spent hours
reading, the "usefullest [days] of my life."

## DICKENS BEGINS AS A JOURNALIST

Four years after taking a law-clerk job, Dickens began his
writing career as a reporter. Once he had mastered shorthand, he set himself up as a freelance reporter near the law
courts and waited to be hired as a recorder of court cases. He
acquired a job on the *Mirror of Parliament,* a paper that reported the daily transactions of the lawmakers, and worked
his way to an advanced position hiring and supervising
other reporters. He earned a reputation for accuracy and
speed in recording speeches of members of Parliament, and
was invited to join the staff of another paper, the *True Sun.*

As a reporter observing the workings of Parliament, he was unimpressed with its red tape; he saw that a few reforms benefited the middle class, but that lawmakers did nothing for the masses of poor whose lives were, as he described, "misery, starvation, unemployment and cholera." Though he himself had acquired some professional and economic success, he still remembered the days in the blacking factory and had compassion for those who worked hard and had almost nothing.

While working at the law office, Dickens had met and fallen in love with Maria Beadnell, a banker's daughter a year older than he. Dickens pursued her diligently, but her parents disapproved. The disappointment of losing Maria renewed old feelings of despair and shame felt so vividly during the days of the blacking factory. At his twenty-first birthday party, Maria rejected him, after which Charles returned her letters, but she kept up a teasing relationship that fed his hopes. When Maria's parents sent her to Paris to finishing school, Charles realized he had no chance to win her love after four years of trying. He vowed he would never again be anyone's plaything. Lacking family wealth or prestige, he would need independent success, and from then on he was determined to have his way.

After 1833 Dickens's determination and hard work brought results. The *Morning Chronicle* hired him as a full-time reporter and soon after added him to the staff of its affiliate, the *Evening Chronicle*. When the *Monthly Magazine* printed, without his name and without paying him, a sketch Dickens had submitted, he was thrilled to see his writing in print. The editors asked for more sketches, which he signed "Boz" for the first time in 1834. Dickens took the name Boz from his family; his little brother Augustus, nicknamed Moses but unable to pronounce the word, called himself Boz. When Dickens was covering plays for the *Evening Chronicle*, he discovered that some of the Boz sketches had been adapted for the stage. Dickens's "sketches" were entertainingly written anecdotes about London people and places. Since the *Monthly Magazine* did not pay him, he quit and wrote street sketches for the *Evening Chronicle*. In addition, he wrote twelve sketches for *Bell's Life in London*. His new success brought him to the attention of writer William Harrison Ainsworth, who introduced Dickens to artist George Cruikshank and publisher John Macrone. In 1836, on Dickens's twenty-fourth birthday, Macrone published *Sketches by Boz,* a two-volume collection of sketches illustrated by Cruikshank.

George Hogarth, Dickens's editor on the *Evening Chronicle,* often invited Dickens to join family gatherings and introduced Dickens to his daughters, all of whom Dickens found charming. On April 2, 1836, he married the oldest daughter, Catherine, called Kate, at St. Luke's Church, Chelsea. When the couple was settled, Catherine's sixteen-year-old sister, Mary, came to live with them; unmarried sisters or brothers' living with a married couple was common practice in Dickens's day. Later, Dickens's brother Fred also lived in their home. Charles and Mary, who had a sweeter disposition than Catherine, developed a close friendship with more understanding than existed between Charles and his wife, who nevertheless bore ten children, seven boys and three girls, between 1837 and 1852.

## FROM SKETCHES TO NOVELS

When *Sketches by Boz* brought good reviews, publishers Chapman and Hall invited Dickens to write, for £14 a month, twenty monthly installments about an imaginary sports club, the Nemrod Club, sketches to be illustrated by Robert Seymour. Dickens, knowing nothing about sports, renegotiated the proposal to focus instead on the travels and investigations of Mr. Pickwick and the imaginary Pickwick Club, illustrated by Hablôt Knight Browne, called Phiz, who became Dickens's illustrator for other works. The first installments from the Pickwick Club were poorly received, until Dickens added the character of Sam Weller in the fourth installment. The addition changed the fortunes of the series from sales of four thousand to forty thousand copies. Biographer Wolf Mankowitz describes the popularity of Pickwick:

> It was read upstairs and downstairs [by all classes], by judges on the bench and the cleaners after them. . . . Critics spoke of Dickens as another Cervantes, poor people shared a shilling copy and read it aloud in groups. A clergyman, having consoled a sick man, heard him mutter behind his back, "Well, thank God, Pickwick will be out in ten days anyway!"

Chapman and Hall sold back issues by the thousands, and they more than doubled Dickens's salary. The installments were published as a book, entitled *Pickwick Papers,* in 1837.

Dickens was "the sudden lion of the town," and offers poured in for children's books, novels, and more sketches.

Dickens accepted an offer to edit the monthly *Bentley's Miscellany* and include in it installments of *Oliver Twist,* to be illustrated by Cruikshank, the illustrator of Boz. The first February 1837 installment garnered great reviews and sold many copies even though it had a more serious tone than *Pickwick.* In *Pickwick,* Dickens presented prison with humor and a mild view; in *Oliver Twist,* he wrote about prison in grave, realistic language. While he was writing the installments for the novel, Mary Hogarth died suddenly. Because Dickens loved Mary as a close friend, he felt such grief he had to take time off. He coped with the loss by taking long walks and horseback rides with John Forster, who had become his friend and agent. Dickens's sadness over Mary's death further strained his relationship with Catherine, who, though she mourned the loss of her sister, was jealous of her husband's affection for Mary. Determined to continue writing, he finished the installments, after which Bentley published *Oliver Twist* in a three-volume book in 1838, the first book to have Dickens's name, not the anonymous "Boz," on the title page.

Before Dickens completed *Oliver Twist* he was already thinking of his next novel, and he traveled with his illustrator Phiz to Yorkshire to research the conditions of boarding schools there. He found maggots, fleas, beatings, and ignorance, schools where illegitimate children were hidden for low fees. At Bowes Academy, run by one-eyed William Shaw, boys were sick, some went blind, and on average one died each year. These schools became the model for Dotheboys Hall in *Nicholas Nickleby,* whose first installment was published in April 1838 while Dickens was still drawing praise from critics for *Oliver Twist.* Of *Nicholas Nickleby,* biographer Edgar Johnson says, "it mingles the sunlight of *Pickwick* with the darkness of *Oliver,*" and "fuses the inexhaustible laughter of *Pickwick* with the somber themes of *Oliver Twist.*" These two books, *Oliver Twist* and *Nicholas Nickleby,* Johnson says, "were clarion peals announcing to the world that in Charles Dickens the rejected and forgotten and misused of the world had a champion." The first installment of *Nicholas Nickleby* sold fifty thousand copies on the first day.

The success of Dickens's books brought him enough

earnings to move up in social class. He bought a house with a gate on Doughty Street in London and traveled within England and abroad. He was invited to join social clubs and literary societies and met other writers—essayist Leigh Hunt and novelists William Thackeray and Edward Bulwer-Lytton. Invitations came to Dickens from the city's cultured elite on the west end of town, but not to Kate, not known for charm or wit. Dickens was greeted by footmen and led up grand staircases to attend breakfasts and dinners at which the educated and famous displayed their skills and amused one another. Mankowitz describes Dickens's reaction to this social class:

> It was a strictly mannered, often cruel world, but Dickens had already learned self-assurance, was a practised mimic of any tone, and felt confident in his intelligence and great gifts: gifts, he soon came to realize, that few of these privileged people had even a tiny part of. That awareness defended him against their insolence or patronization. He was acute enough to see behind the social masks.

As Mankowitz says, Dickens's novels harshly satirize the "masters of material gain and the parasites of materialism, in law courts, the factories and workhouses," but they seldom attack the aristocratic and intellectual elite. He became adviser to one of its members, Angela Burdett Coutts, an heiress who wanted to use money from her two fortunes for social improvement. She took Dickens's advice to fund slum clearance and homes for "fallen women."

Though Dickens's social relations went smoothly, his relations with critics and publishers were often rancorous. Writing about *Oliver Twist,* one critic said that Dickens wrote so much and so fast that he was likely to decline in quality and popularity unless he slowed down. Dickens, angered, vowed, "They shall eat their words." G.K. Chesterton thought perhaps the critics misunderstood Dickens and said, "Dickens has greatly suffered with the critics precisely through this stunning simplicity in his best work," but his disputes with publishers usually involved money and contracts, not the quality of his work. Dickens was inclined to sign a contract that seemed good at the time, then demand more money than the original contract stipulated when sales and the publisher's profits were much larger than expected. In one dispute with the publisher Bentley, Dickens wanted both money and a change in the work contract.

Bentley had published *Oliver Twist,* and contracted with Dickens for two additional novels. Dickens wanted to consider *Oliver Twist* one of the two and then jump to the publishers Chapman and Hall. When the dispute reached a stalemate, Dickens's friend and agent Forster negotiated for him. The determination Dickens had learned from the days at the blacking factory got him what he wanted but left hard feelings with the publisher that Forster was unable to smooth over.

## LITTLE NELL SAVES A WEEKLY

Dickens wanted to be free of the contract with Bentley because he had an idea for a weekly that he wanted Chapman and Hall to fund. Dickens intended *Master Humphrey's Clock* to include a variety of short sketches written by a number of contributors. Responding to the sale of seventy thousand copies of the first issue, Dickens said, "What will the wiseacres say to weekly issues *now?* and what will they say to any of those ten thousand things we shall do together to make 'em writhe and stagger in their shoes." Sales, however, dropped markedly when the public discovered the weekly had no installments by Dickens. Within two weeks, Dickens was serializing *The Old Curiosity Shop,* a travel story about an odd collection of characters. In *The World of Charles Dickens,* Angus Wilson says that this novel

> shows up alarmingly to modern readers the degree of oddity then accepted in a supposedly realistic story—a devilish, fire-drinking dwarf, a little child, an undersized servant maid, a woman (Sally Brass), who is reported as having enlisted as a guardsman or gone down to the docks in male attire, a small boy who stands on his head in mudflats.

It was, however, sweet Little Nell, persecuted by the dwarf Quilp and loved by the honest boy Kit Nubbles, who captured readers' hearts and sent weekly sales above a hundred thousand copies. When Nell neared death, readers deluged the paper with letters pleading that Dickens not let her die. Die she did, nonetheless, in an installment that prompted an outpouring of emotion, as Mankowitz describes:

> Scottish critic Lord Jeffrey was found weeping in his library. 'I'm a great goose to have given way so', he sobbed, 'but I couldn't help it.' [Actor William] Macready, [playwright and poet Walter] Landor, Thomas Carlyle and Edgar Allan Poe were all moved to a similar plight. So was [member of Parliament] Daniel O'Connell, reading on a train journey; he

groaned, 'He should not have killed her', and threw the story out of the window.

Dickens's hold on the attention and sentiment of the public loosened with the weekly installments of his next novel written for *Master Humphrey's Clock*. A historical novel, *Barnaby Rudge* recounts the riots of the poor against Parliament, but Dickens gives the story a more anti-Catholic than anti-Parliament emphasis. The strain of producing weekly installments of two books took a toll on Dickens's health, and he took a year's rest, which publishers Chapman and Hall funded with a salary.

### DICKENS'S VISIT TO AMERICA

During his year off, Dickens and Catherine visited America. They sailed on January 2, 1842, and arrived in Boston to huge crowds wanting to know why Little Nell had to die. He and Catherine visited Boston, Niagara, Philadelphia, St. Louis, and New York City. Wherever he went, crowds surrounded him, cheered, stared, wrung his hand, and clipped fur souvenirs from his coat. He had invitations from every state, from universities, Congress, and all kinds of public and private bodies. He visited orphanages, schools for the blind, reform schools, prisons, and industrial mills. New York published a special edition, the *Extra Boz Herald*, and held a Boz Ball in a ballroom decorated with characters from his books. In a letter to Forster, Dickens wrote:

> I can do nothing that I want to do, go nowhere where I want to go, and see nothing that I want to see. If I turn into the street, I am followed by a multitude. If I stay at home, the house becomes, with callers, like a fair. . . . If I go to a party in the evening, and am so enclosed and hedged about by people, stand where I will, that I am exhausted for want of air. I go to church for quiet, and there is a violent rush to the neighbourhood of the pew I sit in, and the clergyman preaches at *me*. I take my seat in a railroad car, and the very conductor won't leave me alone. I get out at a station, and can't drink a glass of water, without having a hundred people looking down my throat when I open my mouth to swallow. . . . I have no peace, and am in a perpetual worry.

In Washington, D.C., Dickens attended a session of Congress and visited President Tyler, who said little and sat beside a spitoon. To Dickens's amazement, people everywhere—in offices of the state, in courts of law, at parties, in bars, on trains—chewed large wads of tobacco and spit everywhere, "all squirted forth upon the carpet a yellow saliva which quite altered the pattern." Dickens's patience gradually ran out. At one dinner in his honor, after being introduced as a moral reformer and a champion of the downtrodden, Dickens began speaking in the manner expected of him, but midway in his remarks, he switched to the topic of American copyright laws and railed against the unfairness of Americans who made a profit from his works and those of Sir Walter Scott without paying the authors anything. The audience applauded politely, but the next day's papers criticized him for insulting those who had come to honor him. American authors remained silent on the subject, a situation that baffled and rankled Dickens. G.K. Chesterton comments on the English misunderstanding of Americans:

> America is a mystery to any good Englishman; but I think Dickens managed somehow to touch it on a queer nerve. There is one thing, at any rate, . . . that while there is no materialism so crude or so material as American materialism, there is also no idealism so crude or so ideal as American idealism. America will always affect an Englishman as being soft in the wrong place and hard in the wrong place. . . . Some beautiful ideal runs through this people, but it runs aslant.

After four months of tours, crowds, and little privacy, Dickens left New York harbor on June 7, 1842, to sail for home, his children and friends, and his writing.

Before beginning his next novel, Dickens recorded his impressions of his American visit in *American Notes*. In polite tones, he praised many features of American life (and remained silent about copyright laws). America had, however, failed to live up to Dickens's expectations; its slavery, its business practices, its sensational journalism, and the manners of its people offended him. The book brought Dickens £1,000 toward the cost of the trip, but it brought him an array of adjectives in American newspapers—"coarse, vulgar, impudent, superficial, narrow-minded, conceited cockney, flimsy, childish, trashy, contemptible." He was less polite in his next book. After several installments of *Martin Chuzzlewit* sold poorly, Dickens hoped to increase sales by sending Martin to America. With none of the polite restraint shown in *American Notes*, Dickens expressed his impatience with America in harsh humor through the character of Mrs. Gamp, a brutalized victim of the society in which Mr. Pecksniff rules with unctuous hypocrisy. The Americans were angry, the British disappointed by its bitter tone, and Dickens's publishers reduced his year-off salary.

## RESTLESSNESS AND TRAVEL

The year following his American visit, 1843, began a period of restlessness for Dickens. In a row with Chapman and Hall over salary, Dickens lost his temper and threatened to find a new publisher, but Christmas was coming soon and he did not act. He calmed down and wrote "A Christmas Carol" in time to be published before the holidays, and hosted a big Christmas party at his home. Georgina Hogarth, daughter of George Hogarth, who was as sweet as Mary had been, came to live in the Dickens home. After the holidays, Dickens took his family and servants to Italy, stopping first in Genoa and renting a house from which he could hear Genoa's constantly chiming bells. He used the opportunity to write another Christmas story, entitled "The Chimes," which became the second in a series of annual Christmas stories. In the following years, he wrote "The Cricket on the Hearth," "The Battle of Life," and "The Haunted Man" for publication just before the holidays. Before returning to England, he and Kate toured southern Italy, where he came to appreciate the manners and language of the Italians but grew to dislike the Catholic Church, which was, he thought, "a political arm against the poor and ignorant." Unlike his American trip, this trip was private and much more satisfying. When he returned to England in 1846, he started a new liberal paper, *Daily News,* during a political turmoil over the Corn Laws. When the first issue came off the press, ten thousand Londoners wanted to see what Dickens had said, as did thousands around the rest of the country. But once the paper was successfully established, Dickens lost patience with the details of publication and turned it over to Forster after seventeen issues.

Dickens became a familiar figure in London and a comic but difficult character in his home. A man of medium height who appeared small, he had thick brown hair, a mustache and beard, a large expressive mouth, and bright, active eyes that darted back and forth, taking in the details around him. His nervous and delicate manner belied a rather steely personality. He wore flashy waistcoats and velvet coats in public and liked to be looked at if the looks were admiring. Personally, he fussed over little things and directed his whims to be acted on instantly: If the house was too quiet at night, everyone had to get up; if it was too noisy, all had to be quiet. G.K. Chesterton said of Dickens, "His private life consisted of one tragedy and ten thousand comedies." His marriage was a failure, but he loved his children, and filled their home with energy, with daily pranks and practical jokes.

## PERSONAL AND PROFESSIONAL TURNING POINTS

The mid-1840s marked a turning point both in Dickens's personal life and in his novels. Unhappy in his marriage, he developed undisciplined and unhealthy habits in his daily routines. His discontent spurred him to go to Lausanne, Switzerland, to start a new novel, *Dombey and Son,* his last farce. Like all of Dickens's first novels, which are primarily farces, *Dombey* is filled with caricatures who could not exist anywhere; the novels that followed have more realistic characters who could live everywhere. *Dombey* attacks the class system and moral pestilence that Dickens believed corrupted English society. He believed that the aristocracy perpetuated itself by taking advantage of "the pure, weak good nature" of the people.

If *Dombey* is the last of the first novels, *David Copperfield* is the transition novel. Dickens got the idea for the title by reversing his initials. It is his most autobiographical book and his favorite, about which he said, "I really think I have done it ingeniously and with a very complicated interweaving of truth and fiction." He tells the story of David in the first person and makes memory an important part of the theme, memories so personal that at one point he temporarily stopped writing because he felt sick and weak and shed tears for days. Writing *David Copperfield* helped to heal some of Dickens's wounds: "I can never approach the book with perfect composure it had such perfect possession of me when I wrote it." From the first installment in May 1849, the book was a success with the public. Novelist William Thackeray said, "By jingo it's beautiful. . . . Those inimitable Dickens touches which make such a great man of him. . . . There are little words and phrases in his book that are like personal benefits to his readers. . . . Bravo Dickens." And yet after the successful completion of this novel, Dickens was still restless and filled with nervous energy, which he directed toward production of plays.

As early as 1836, Dickens was interested in plays, but he had little success as a dramatist. His interest continued, however, in the form of amateur theatricals, farces Dickens and his family performed for friends at annual Twelfth Night celebrations in his home. Each year these productions became more elaborate until he offered them publicly and used the profits for charity. In 1847 he organized a theatrical company for his charity plays, arranged a benefit tour of the play *Every Man in His Humor,* and gave the profits to a budding but poor playwright. The next year the company produced *The Merry Wives of Windsor* to buy Shakespeare's birthplace in Stratford-on-Avon as a national monument. As the production of charity plays grew and audiences increased, Dickens hired professional actresses Mary Boyle and Ellen Ternan. In 1852 the company performed in thirteen cities and put on a performance for Queen Victoria, all profits going to the Guild of Literature and Art.

Amid his busy schedule of writing books and producing plays, Dickens leased a larger house in Tavistock Square in a more fashionable area of London, but first contracted to reconstruct, redecorate, and refurnish it before the family moved in. While waiting for the work to be done, he was too agitated to work; he said, "I sit down between whiles to think of a new story, and, as it begins to grow, such a torment of desire to be anywhere but where I am . . . takes hold of me, that it is like being *driven away.*" He settled down, however, after he had moved into the Tavistock home and started *Bleak House.* The first novel of the second, more realistic phase, *Bleak House* centers around a legal issue that typified the way the courts handled cases for prisoners of Chancery. Dickens parallels the slow pace of the courts to the coming and going of the indifferent political parties, satirically called Boodle and Coodle. From the first chapter, fog covers the whole London world of Chancery, the dark, murky atmosphere in which Dickens exposes the corruptions and ineptitudes of government and the courts. The first issue of *Bleak House* exceeded the sales of *David Copperfield* by ten thousand copies.

In 1850 Dickens started and edited a weekly called *Household Words,* a publication of short articles and tidbits written by a variety of contributors. Though Dickens exercised firm control over the editing of contributors' work, he gave many young writers an opportunity for valuable training. Subject matter covered a wide range: public education, campaigns against social abuses, entertainment, fiction, and humor. Two weeks after its first issue, a monthly news supplement was added, the *Household Narrative of Current Events.* The weekly carried explanations of scientific and technological discoveries, brief biographies of many historical figures, reviews of new and old books, travel tips, and Dickens's installments of *A Child's History of England.* Since three out of four people in England could read, Dickens wanted the weekly to appeal to all social classes. When circulation began to decline after more than two years of regular publication, Dickens propped up sales with a new book, *Hard Times,* in which he uses places to portray two opposing views. Coketown represents cold, rational industrialism and the Circus represents warmth, intuition, and humanity; in the end, the natural world of Sissy Jupe and the Circus people is the only hope. Before writing this book about the materialistic laws of supply and demand, the system of high profits and cheap labor preached by utilitarians, Dickens toured the cotton mills of Lancashire and interviewed striking cotton workers in Preston.

## PUBLIC SUCCESS AND PRIVATE SADNESS

As a result of the reforms Dickens advocated in *Household Words,* he was sought as a public speaker and lecturer; out of these appearances he developed public readings from his works. He began with readings of "A Christmas Carol" and donated the proceeds to poor workers. He added other works, cut the excerpts and wrote stage directions, and took his readings throughout England, Scotland, and Ireland to audiences up to two thousand. Though he did not need the money and the exertion of performance strained his health, he liked the stimulation he received from the audiences. The next year, he hired a personal valet and an agent to help him with forty-two performances in Birmingham and Ireland. In 1867 he planned a hundred readings for an American tour. He had large, sell-out audiences in Boston, New York, Philadelphia, Baltimore, and Washington. But after seventy-six performances, Dickens's health was failing and he had to go home. In 1868 he went on a farewell reading tour in London, Ireland, and Scotland, but grew more and more exhausted with each performance. His agent Dolby, who urged him to quit, described Dickens as a man with "the iron will of a demon and the tender pity of an angel." At every reading, Dickens insisted that a certain number of good seats be sold for a small amount to the poor, believing that those he had spent his life championing should be able to hear what he said.

For many years, Dickens's public life had been a series of successes, but his private life was marked by numerous sad events. In 1848 his sister Fanny died of tuberculosis, followed by the death of her crippled son. Following the birth of their third daughter, Kate had a nervous breakdown. Shortly after Kate recovered, Dickens's father, John, died, and the baby, Dora Annie, became ill and died before she was a year old. Over the years, Dickens's relationship with Kate had continued to deteriorate, and when Dickens flirted with other women and gave them his attention, Kate, cowed by her famous and brilliant husband, withdrew further. During one of the public-reading tours, Kate left him. Dickens blamed himself:

> It is not only that she makes me uneasy and unhappy, but that I make her so too—and much more so . . . but we are strangely ill-assorted for the bond there is between us. God knows she would have been a thousand times happier if she had married another kind of man, and that her avoidance of this destiny would have been at least equally good for us both. I am often cut to the heart by thinking what a pity it is, for her own sake, that I ever fell in her way.

When Kate left with one of the children, Georgina Hogarth stayed on and ran the household as she had been doing for some years. In addition to his other problems, several of Dickens's brothers, who managed money as irresponsibly as their father had done, asked Dickens for financial help. While personal problems made him impatient and irritable, they never depleted his energy and enthusiasm for his work.

Dickens's whirlwind of plays, readings, serials, family, friends, travels, and new houses never seemed to die down. By chance, Dickens learned that he could buy Gad's Hill, the "castle" from his childhood, when he discovered that one of the contributors to *Household Words*, Eliza Lynn, owned it and wanted to sell. "I used to look at it [Gad's Hill] as a wonderful Mansion (which God knows it is not), when I was a very odd little child with the first faint shadows of all my books in my head," he said. He had it renovated and enlarged and brought his family there for the summer of 1857. Dickens was spending more of his time with younger people now—his children, the staff of *Household Words*, and actors from the charity plays. He particularly enjoyed a friendship with Wilkie Collins, a young writer on the staff, and traveled with him to the Lake District and Paris. And his attraction to young Ellen Ternan, with whom he had acted in many plays, grew to serious infatuation.

## NEW NOVELS FOR THE MAGAZINES

Dickens's major accomplishment in the last two decades of his life was the writing of six novels and part of a seventh that constitute the second phase of his career. After *Bleak House* and *Hard Times* came *Little Dorrit*, a serial novel in which Dickens attacks the cynicism, despair, and victim attitude that existed in all levels of society. It has few saints and few villains but many gray characters—bad people with redeeming qualities and good people with sinister motives. Little Dorrit, whose girlhood is affected, as Dickens's was, by a father imprisoned for debts, grows up to lead a useful, happy life. Before writing another novel, Dickens had a fight with his publisher of fourteen years, Bradbury and Evans. In the outcome, Dickens took *Household Words*, renamed it *All the Year Round*, and went back to publishers Chapman and Hall. The first serial novel published in the renamed weekly was *A Tale of Two Cities*, Dickens's story version of Thomas Carlyle's account of the French Revolution and the last book illustrated by Phiz. In this book, Dickens explores the theme of renunciation, redemption, and resurrection through the character of Sydney Carton, who offers to die in a convicted man's place.

A year later, Dickens explores the same theme of renunciation, redemption, and resurrection in *Great Expectations*. The main character, Pip, goes from the country to London and back, during which he meets eccentric characters and discovers that multiple strands of his life are interwoven. During the interim between *Great Expectations* and Dickens's next novel, Chapman and Hall published a collection of pieces from *All the Year Round* entitled *The Uncommercial Traveller*, the same title used for a second collection four years later. The next novel, *Our Mutual Friend*, appeared in monthly installments for a year and a half, beginning in May 1864. It is a modern novel, set in Dickens's mid-Victorian England, in which he anticipates the nature of declining Victorianism. He portrays a society so corrupt that money, which Dickens symbolizes as huge dustheaps, has become the measure of human worth. Angus Wilson says of *Our Mutual Friend*, "What is so extraordinary is that the tired Dickens should so nearly capture this world of the future, this world only glimpsed by a few beneath the seeming-solid surface of the sixties." The last novel, *The Mystery of Edwin Drood,* set in a small cathedral town, involves the upper-middle, professional class. In the six parts that Dickens wrote before he died, there is an unsolved murder, and critics have argued that its theme involves the forces of law against evil.

## DECLINING HEALTH AND DEATH

Dickens's health was in decline for the last five years of his life. After a mild stroke in 1865, he drove himself to exhaustion on his reading tours. In March 1870, he gave his final public reading at St. James Hall. At the end, when his voice weakened, two thousand people rose to their feet, and he returned to the stage. Tears falling down his cheeks, he said, "From these garish lights I now vanish for ever more, with a heartfelt, grateful, respectful, affectionate farewell," and he kissed his hands to the audience and was gone. In late spring, he went to Gad's Hill to work on *Edwin Drood,* but he seemed to know the end was near when he told his daughter Katey on her last visit that he had high hopes for the book if he lived to finish it. On June 8, he worked all day rather than following his usual routine of working only in the morning. When he stood up from the dinner table that evening, he collapsed and was put on the sofa. He lay quietly, breathing heavily, until six o'clock the next evening, June 9, 1870, when he died at the age of fifty-eight. On June 14, his body was brought to Westminster Abbey, and after a simple service, he was laid to rest in Poet's Corner, a section of the church where honored writers are buried. Thousands of people filed past the grave left open for the public until it was full to overflowing with flowers.

# CHAPTER 1

# Major Themes in Dickens's Novels

READINGS ON
CHARLES DICKENS

# Dickens as Reformer and Moralist

Joseph Gold

Joseph Gold explores the way Dickens portrays morbid experiences with optimism and humor. According to Gold, Dickens sees that an unjust society creates a dismal life for many people, but many of them consistently display love and moral behavior in spite of injustices, therein giving reason for optimism, humor, and moral vision. Joseph Gold has taught English at the University of Manitoba and the University of Waterloo in Canada. He is the compiler of *The Stature of Dickens: A Centenary Bibliography* and author of *In the Name of English.*

Dickens' canon can be divided along roughly chronological lines into major phases of preoccupation. The first, which I would call Anatomy of Society, describes those earlier novels that centre mainly on the attempt of character to be happily integrated into a hostile and destructive society. The emphasis here is on a society that ought to be radically altered so as to permit the integration of the individual and an end to injustice and cruelty. The second phase could be described as Autonomy of Self, to indicate how the later novels concentrate on the individual character and on the search for freedom and for answers within himself, regardless of how society swirls around him. Society becomes more and more an abstraction and self becomes more and more a concrete reality in Dickens' work. The two divisions are obviously crude yet they serve to give the direction of my reading of the subject.

In other words the vision of a world built on love and wisdom, on uncorrupted or at least redeemed perception, is also a vision of whole, redeemed individuals. Tortured minds and distorted perceptions breed a sick society. The optimism

Excerpted from Joseph Gold, *Charles Dickens: Radical Moralist* (Minneapolis: University of Minnesota Press, 1972). Reprinted by permission of the author.

and humour of which House[1] speaks are the signs of the moral visionary; the "intimate understanding of morbid and near-morbid psychology" is the sign of the radical reformer who sees that it is individual corruption and fragmentation that lie as the obstacle before the attainment of his vision. . . .

The happy endings of Dickens' novels turn out to be not so happy, or at least ambivalent, on closer inspection. Dickens seems in every case to be clearly indicating his sophisticated awareness that we have a choice as to the kind of endings we will write for every story, his or our own. What he did explicitly for *Great Expectations* seems implicitly done elsewhere. Pickwick creates his own garden society, but "Messrs. Dodson and Fogg, continue in business, from which they realize a large income, and in which they are universally considered among the sharpest of the sharp" *(Pickwick Papers)*. Oliver finds a world of love and family harmony, again in a country setting, but Dick has died and Nancy and Fagin have been "butchered." As Amy Dorrit and Arthur become "inseparable and blessed" they move still through a world in which the "arrogant and the froward and the vain, fretted, and chafed, and made their usual uproar" *(Little Dorrit)*. Every novel has this dual quality, this double-vision ending, and it is here that one may see just how Dickens blended the humourist, the moralist and the social, radical reformer-psychologist. . . .

## DICKENS AS REFORMER, MORALIST, RADICAL, OR VISIONARY?

George Orwell has pointed out that Dickens was not a reformer in any conventional sense:

> Whatever else Dickens may have been, he was not a hole-and-corner soul-saver, the kind who thinks that the world will be perfect if you amend a few by-laws and abolish a few anomalies.[2]

. . . He was rather a moralist. "The truth is that Dickens' criticism of society is almost exclusively moral." If Dickens was not a conventional reformer, what sort was he? . . .

Not only did Orwell see that the moralist and the radical meet in Dickens but he also managed a penetrating glimpse into the method by which reform could be envisioned by the moralist. "It seems that in every attack Dickens makes upon

---

1. Critic Humphry House cites the problem of reconciling Dickens's understanding of morbid psychology with his optimism and humor.   2. George Orwell, "Charles Dickens," in *Critical Essays* (London: Secker & Warburg, 1946)

society he is always pointing to a change of spirit rather than a change of structure." House, too, understands that the moralist-radical might be a visionary closer in some ways to Blake[3] than to Marx.[4] "He [Dickens] made . . . a complete world with a life and vigour and idiom of its own, quite unlike any other world there has ever been." Orwell shows that it is possible to reduce this vision to a single incredibly facile proposition. "His whole 'message' is one that at first glance looks like an enormous platitude: If men would behave decently the world would be decent.". . .

The universal sympathy and pleasure evoked by Dickens' world may depend most on this persistent and profound human desire for personal and social harmony. It is a compulsion that senses that alterations in social structure are a pathetic embodiment of the kind of transformation really wanted; a desire which, for this very reason, puts a high value on the image of more humane social structures. Images of a protected and happier world are the reminder and the reinforcement of a desire for a more profound and total redemption.

Orwell's word "decent" reveals how much remains to be done in Dickens' criticism. This study proposes that such a search makes necessary the analysis of evil that gives the novels so much of their extraordinary and memorable force and colour. To my mind no other body of prose (or poetry for that matter, with the inevitable exception of Shakespeare) presents such a searching and vivid and indeed entertaining examination of modes of evil and error or of the psychology of those who are distorted by destructive passions or mistaken values. . . .

Dickens became through his career increasingly and more deeply concerned with questions implicit in the early works. There are no changes in the author's convictions from Pickwick to Boffin. But there is no John Rokesmith[5] in the early novel, nor could there be, for while Dickens saw perfectly from the start what good and evil looked like, in all their guises, he did not explore their underlying psychology until much later. The question of identity, of self-definition and of truth or distortion in individual personality, increasingly becomes the preoccupation. The necessity for self-

3. British poet William   4. German philosopher and economist Karl   5. Boffin and John Rokesmith are characters in *Our Mutual Friend.*

awareness, not "in the letter" as it is possessed by Ralph Nickleby, but in the spirit as it is acquired by later characters, becomes more and more the central moral force of Dickens' fiction. Self-deceit, illusion and delusion, rationalization and wish-fulfillment are explored in the Dickens canon with ever-increasing perception and persistence. We are shown self-questioning, the analysis of motivation, the search for the self, the questioning of the past. Only through these means, Dickens comes to say, can the individual reconcile himself to his humanity and thus overcome his weakest impulses and compulsions, and subsequently the evils of his society.

The world of automatic response in *Oliver Twist* and of acting and pretension in *Nicholas Nickleby* becomes a world of more intense individual concern and interaction in *Great Expectations* and *Little Dorrit* and *Our Mutual Friend.* Thus it is that the great last novels are more complex and earnest and difficult and "dark." They penetrate more deeply to seek answers to questions inherent from the start. In the search for these answers it seems to happen that Dickens discovers the object of his search to be not social evil at all, but the everlasting existential questions that great art always leads to. It is impossible not to regard Dick's death, at the end of *Oliver Twist,* as connected with social causes, with the workhouse world and inhumane treatment.

Increasingly, however, we become aware of a deepening tragic tone. The situations become cosmic and human rather than social. Steerforth dies, Ham dies, Estella suffers, Pip learns, Mrs. Clennam festers, Wrayburn is nearly murdered, not because of bad institutions or inhumane laws. These are personal events bred from the nature of humanity itself. It is in the struggle to understand and portray these complexities that the canon grows richer and more profound. Given that one is born and is human and will die; given that one has a past, parents, class and personality; given that we are driven, deluded, tossed by emotions and desires, how can we move to some personal peace and redemption, to love, to forgiveness, to reconciliation with our humanity?

## DICKENS CHARTS A MORAL COURSE

The moralist must believe that such a peace is possible; that if we have a bad and a good self, a bad and a good angel, as do many of Dickens' characters, a meaningful struggle between them can happen and a victory be achieved. The moralist starts from faith, from a hard foundation of belief that what we do and what we are matters and can be changed. Dickens, as moralist, moves with increasing penetration to the expansion of how this may be done. The novelist ultimately has only models, the philosopher, abstractions. The novelist shows us what moral redemption might look like as perceived by his vision. There is not, in fiction, a moral method to be followed. It is not a theology. Yet more and more Dickens strives to present such a method. His moral vision becomes clearer and more forceful with every work and his desire to be explicit becomes more evident, but this path to goodness, this pilgrims' way, remains elusive. Rokesmith's interior monologue and self-analysis is not, finally, as powerful as the novel's metaphor of drowning and rebirth, the explicit affirmation that change and love and vision are possible. It is the affirmation itself that finally grasps the reader's mind and heart. What never changes in Dickens is the conviction of the value of human love; the methods of expressing that conviction become ever more complex. . . .

No single book, or library of books, can begin to touch the vastness of Dickens' novels, the hundreds of characters, places, plots, descriptions, observations; the style, the language, the diction, the structure, the mode, the mood; the history, the sociology, the psychology; the influences, the sources, the allusions, the borrowings, the echoes. Each work of criticism must inevitably, furthermore, distort its subject. Dickens was not a philosopher or historian. When we abstract we no longer have Dickens, for his "message," or more properly, his vision, is its embodiment in fiction. Rather we should regard the critic as throwing some tinted illumination on the work which, while it does not itself change, may thereafter appear to the reader in a new and interesting light.

[Psychoanalyst] Erich Fromm has said that loving is an art, the most important art of all, and that this art takes its meaning, like all arts, from its being practised, from being a process, yielding rewards in the very act of loving and being in process. I would suggest that loving is part of an even more demanding art, the art of being human. . . .

To explore the sources and nature of one's humanity, to seek the fringes of one's own human possibilities, to examine the quality of all aspects of one's relations to man and nature, to sound the depths of one's own core of being, these are the characteristics of the art of being human. I would like to show that Dickens is the celebrant of this art. He was the writer who consciously directed the power of his imagination to the creation of a mythology of society. Dickens devoted his creative life to the exploration of social experience, from the fully human being to the fragmented and partially human creature. His novels constitute an unparalleled presentation.

## DICKENS RELEVANT TODAY

Perhaps we need Dickens today more than ever, for his writing produces that sense of liberating courage, that vision of human complexity and possibility that restores our faith in our own humanity. Whatever else his work may be, however we may disagree on particulars, it is unmistakably a celebration. In this sense, as well as in many others, Dickens is joyously existential in his vision. It is because of Dickens' incredible energy, his manifest engagement with the people and action of his novels and his vision of individual possibility, which when realized or even glimpsed can alone produce a society of a different quality, that I am led to think of his work as a comic quest.

It is comic in its faith in the redeemed society peopled by whole human beings; it is a quest characterized by a mocking castigation *en route* of a frenetic society and the fragmented individuals who sustain it. A comic quest is a journey of the imagination undertaken by one who believes that

> There are dark shadows on the earth, but its lights are stronger in the contrast. Some men, like bats or owls, have better eyes for the darkness than for the light. We, who have no such optical powers, are better pleased to take our last parting look at the visionary companions of many solitary hours, when the brief sunshine of the world is blazing full upon them. (*Pickwick Papers*)

This "brief sunshine of the world" has, by the last complete novel, become the illumination of the individual face and soul, redeemed by love and brought to life by giving up all the illusions of "Society."

> "Now my wife is something nearer to my heart, Mortimer, than Tippins [Society] is, and I owe her a little more than I owe to Tippins, and I am rather prouder of her than I ever was of Tippins. Therefore, I will fight it out to the last gasp, with her and for her, here in the open field. . . ." The glow that shone upon him as he spoke the words so irradiated his fea-

tures, that he looked, for the time, as though he had never been mutilated. (*Our Mutual Friend*)

This study is an attempt to trace the fictional journey, the quest, from Dickens' perception of the "brief sunshine of the world" to the individual's irradiated face, to a love that can transform the living dead "as though he had never been mutilated." It is every man's quest for meaning. Dickens explores evil without compromise, but he provides us with images of courage and faith. He shows us that more often than not life is neither easy, pretty nor happy, but he also convinces us that it is endlessly entertaining and even, by the end of the canon, meaningful. We can, he says, redeem ourselves by this perception.

Our experience of our own world is not only more than enough, it is all that there is. When we have seen this and have shed all the illusions that distract us from this perception, we are reconciled to our own imaginations and the materials to be perceived. We lose our sense of alienation. We are living instead of thinking about living, and our world becomes infinitely fascinating. It is while we are fascinated, while we are moved by compassion, while we are part of what we see, that we are redeemed. We have left the world of time and entered eternity now. Dickens shows us that the world may be perceived as he perceives it in his fiction. This is the fact of his fiction, one supposes of all great art. Its existence proves its point. We are converted into believers willy-nilly. Dickens could have done this without creating any characters in his fiction who also come to this perception. Had this been the case he would have been a great compassionate satirist, with a kind of Chaucerian detachment, creating a world in which no one perceives what the creator perceives. But the moralist in Dickens would not permit him to remain so detached and he adds to his fiction a whole range of characters who become in their turn joyful, compassionate creators of worlds.

Once we have seen the mythological force of this fiction we may lose our fear of identification with these characters, from Pickwick and the Cheerybles to Amy Dorrit and the Golden Dustman. These characters are the artists of being human; they create whole worlds. It is our inadequacy, not their unreality, that makes us so shy of their love and compassion. Strangely enough it is the "good" people in Dickens who have most frequently run foul of the critics. Even Santayana,[6] one of the most sympathetic readers, confesses to this inadequacy, but he is humble and wise enough to see it as his failure and not the author's:

> I must confess, though the fault is mine and not his, that sometimes his absoluteness is too much for me. When I come to the death of little Nell, or to What the Waves were always Saying, or even to the incorrigible perversities of the pretty Dora, I skip. I can't take my liquor neat in such draughts, and my inner man says to Dickens, Please don't. But then I am a coward in so many ways! There are so many things in this world that I skip, as I skip the undiluted Dickens!

Many people have the same difficulty with children and the child's perception as do many readers with the loving, compassionate or playful characters of Dickens' novels, and for similar reasons. Indeed, Dickens himself knew this and provided children a central rôle in his fiction, not simply because their perception was valuable to the moralist in him, but because he wanted to expose and explore the inadequacies of those who are alienated from or threatened by children. Blake found the image of the child and the child in adult society equally valuable for his mythology.

The moralist as artist is someone who believes in and reveals to us our own possibilities for living more meaningfully. The reformer is someone who wants to see a different society appear by some means or other. When these two figures meet in one, as they did in Dickens, they produce a visionary who sees that society is after all the product of our perception of it. Enlighten our perception, free our imagination, and the society we know must disappear, dissolve and be replaced by a world of grace: this is what the fiction comes to say. Dickens is not concerned with the philosophical question of whether such a world is possible. He makes it happen in his art. There are few artists who leave one with the astonished sense that until we saw with their eyes, until they held their world up for us, we never realized how interesting, how fantastic and finally how ordered, our own had been all along.

6. professor, philosopher, and writer George

# Prison Experiences in Dickens's Novels

A.O.J. Cockshut

A.O.J. Cockshut analyzes Dickens's use of prisons in his novels. According to Cockshut, Dickens describes prison from an insider's view that reveals the prisoner's feelings about confinement. Dickens presents a wide range of attitudes. For example, in *Pickwick Papers*, Pickwick voluntarily goes to prison rather than pay a fine, and as Dickens describes him, he is admired for his stand and lives in luxury and comfort during his stay. In *Great Expectations*, Dickens treats prison life seriously, using it as a symbol of all life's suffering. Cockshut concludes that for Dickens prison experience is a metaphor that reflects life's adventure, its fear and pain, and its comfortable familiarity. A.O.J. Cockshut has taught nineteenth-century literature at Oxford University. He is the author of numerous books on literature and religion, including *Anthony Trollope* and *Anglican Attitudes*.

The paramount importance of prisons in Dickens's imaginative life hardly needs to be demonstrated. It is not merely that his father was imprisoned for debt, and that four or five of his books deal with the subject at length, while several others treat it more briefly. Without any biographical reconstructions or laborious statistical statements, every attentive reader is aware that the prison is a dominating image in his work. . . .

For example, in *The Old Curiosity Shop* Little Nell's grandfather is afraid of being forcibly separated from her. This is how the fear presents itself to his mind:

> They will shut me up in a stone room, dark and cold, and chain me up to the wall, Nell, flog me with whips.

He has committed no crime, but for many of Dickens's characters, as for the author himself, the image of the prison is

Excerpted from A.O.J. Cockshut, *The Imagination of Charles Dickens* (New York: New York University Press, 1962). Copyright ©1962 by A.O.J. Cockshut. Reprinted by permission of the author.

always waiting to well up into the mind in moments of crisis. Similarly, other institutions, such as dark and forbidding houses, or workhouses, or schools readily acquire the prison atmosphere. Even voluntary prisoners like Clennam's mother and Miss Havisham may develop all the mental characteristics of people confined by force, and the invisible bonds may be more permanent than the prison walls which sometimes, as in the case of Mr. Dorrit, admit of release.

Several books move between the poles of two kinds of imprisonment as if to suggest that there is ultimately no escape. *Oliver Twist* begins with the "charitable" workhouse imprisonment of Oliver, and ends with Fagin's condemned cell. *A Tale of Two Cities* begins with a royalist prison and ends with a revolutionary one. In *Little Dorrit* this simple idea of the return of the prison is treated with greater subtlety until the prison seems to be everywhere. . . .

In reading Dickens we are always seeing the prison from the inside. The primary thing is never the prison as a legal enactment, or a social problem, but an experience, which we are compelled to share. Apparent exceptions only confirm this point, as when Little Dorrit is locked out of the Marshalsea. She is locked out of her home, and so spends the night more aware than usual of the fact that she belongs nowhere else. . . .

## THE IMAGE OF PRISON IN *PICKWICK PAPERS*

The first significant version of the prison image occurs in *Pickwick Papers*, which, as everybody knows, is the embodiment of a genuine and important, but not very profound aspect of Dickens's nature—the clownish, jolly, vulgar, superficially generous. Even if the prison was a dominating idea for him, he might have been expected to ignore it for once. He did not do that, but he allowed it to appear in deceptive and unreal guise. Mr. Pickwick's imprisonment is, in almost every respect, the opposite of normal. He goes to prison voluntarily, because he refuses on principle to pay damages that are too small to impair his fortune. While he is there he lives in luxury, is comfortable, and is able to occupy himself as he likes. He is not disgraced, but is admired for his fortitude; he retains the affection of his friends and the disinterested loyalty of his servant. He is not required to mingle with the wretched, dirty and poverty-stricken prisoners on the "other side," but when he decides out of pure kindness to go among them for a time, he witnesses, but without any vengeful feelings, the degradation of his old enemy, Jingle. He pities and patronises the wretched, and even, at one point, most improbably of all (for he has led a sheltered life and is old and fat) holds his own in physical combat with a younger man.

Finally, after a short period of imprisonment, he is able to secure release while maintaining his dignity, and to take pity on his unjust accuser. In fact, Mr. Pickwick's imprisonment is a kind of triumphal progress, a vast moral victory gained at very little cost. And all this, of course, is just what we should expect. The whole book is written in a kind of euphoria; the dangers and pains and difficulties of life are no more than a humorous and exhilarating obstacle race in which ultimate success is certain. But one may, in such a euphoric mood, feel compelled to recall former fears and worries, to prove to oneself how easily one can now conquer them. So the appearance of the prison here, though it is only a prison physically and not psychologically, is still significant. The prison in *Pickwick Papers* represents an early and false attempt to scotch what would afterwards prove to be an intractable preoccupation. In the context of Dickens's whole career the gay prison scenes in it are very sad. Dickens was in the position of a drunken debtor outlining his brilliant plans for making a fortune.

## A CONFLICTING ATTITUDE TOWARD PRISON IN *OLIVER TWIST*

In *Oliver Twist,* written a year or two later, a new, but still unsatisfactory attempt is made upon the problem. Oliver's birth in the workhouse, which has sufficiently grim implications, is partly shuffled off with the uneasy facetiousness of passages like this:

> Although I am not disposed to maintain that the being born in a workhouse is in itself the most fortunate and enviable circumstance that can possibly befall a human being, I do mean to say that in this particular instance, it was the best thing for Oliver Twist that could possibly have occurred. The fact is, that there was considerable difficulty in inducing Oliver to take upon himself the office of respiration—a troublesome practice, but one which custom has rendered necessary to our easy existence; and for some time he lay gasping. ... Now if, during this brief period, Oliver had been surrounded by careful grandmothers, anxious aunts, experienced nurses, and doctors of profound wisdom, he would most inevitably and indubitably have been killed in no time.

There being nobody by, however, but a pauper old woman, who was rendered rather misty by an unwonted allowance of beer; and a parish surgeon who did such matters by contract; Oliver and nature fought the point between them.

This passage occurs in the book's third paragraph, and it shows straight away that Dickens has not settled his own attitude to his subject. To describe a lonely boy's unhappy childhood in this tone throughout would be heartless and superficial. But, of course, the tone rapidly changes, and afterwards oscillates between this facetiousness and a pathos that tends to a blurred, exaggerated effect. . . .

The emotional incoherence of the author, at this stage, is very obviously reflected in Oliver himself. He is at one moment a snivelling child, and at another a formidable delinquent and home worker. At other times again he is not very far from being a polished man of the world:

"And consider, ma'am," said Oliver, as the tears forced themselves into his eyes, despite his efforts to the contrary: "oh! consider how young and good she is, and what pleasure and comfort she gives to all about her. I am sure—certain—quite certain—that, for your sake, who are so good yourself, and for her own; for the sake of all she makes so happy; she will not die. Heaven will never let her die so young."

It is obvious from passages like this that no serious thought has been given to the practical effects of being educated in a workhouse and a thieves' kitchen. And the failure is particularly startling if one remembers Dickens's habitual mastery of strange popular idioms—in Mrs. Gamp, for instance, and Sam Weller. And so, though gloomier and outwardly more authentic than in *Pickwick Papers,* the prison remains psychologically unreal.

On the other hand, no one would call *Oliver Twist* a falsely cheerful book. It conveys an impression of horror which every reader remembers when he may have forgotten most of the details. This horror is largely unexplained; the stagy plot is inadequate to it. The book is like a continuous and unsuccessful attempt to pin down, externalise and face the overwhelming nightmares of childhood. And of course the attempt ends in a prison.

The account of Fagin in the condemned cell is certainly vivid and memorable and it is not easy to say just what is wrong with it. But a clue may be found in such a passage as this:

"The dreadful walls of Newgate, which have hidden so

much misery and such unspeakable anguish, not only from the eyes, but, too often, and too long from the thoughts, of men, never held so dread a spectacle as that," i.e. as Fagin sitting alone. This solitary reference to the misery and anguish of Newgate is perfunctory, and is, in any case, out of key with its context, for this prison is presented neither as a social problem nor as a symbol, but as a just punishment of evil. Fagin ceases to be a recognisable member of the criminal class, and becomes a kind of hellish scapegoat. (Cruickshank's famous drawing, in which the condemned Fagin does not look human at all, is entirely in the spirit of the text.) The problem of his guilt, the tricky concepts of crime and punishment are shelved, and instead his execution provides a rather cheap catharsis, a thrill followed by peace. It is almost as if the world's evil falters when the master of evil is killed. If *Pickwick Papers* offers us the prison as quite a jolly place after all, here we have the prison as necessary for the control of vermin. And there is an element of dishonesty in this for the deep thrill derived from contemplating the punishment is not admitted. It only serves to obscure at the end the book's deepest preoccupation—the irrational fears of childhood.

## PRISON INTERNALIZED IN *A TALE OF TWO CITIES*

In *A Tale of Two Cities* Dickens caused two of the dominating images of his literary life to clash. The crowd makes war on the prison. In these passages we are aware of a very deep excitement in the author, as if this was his own private version of the meeting of irresistible force and immovable object. . . . I turn now to the prisons of *A Tale of Two Cities*. If examined in association with *Oliver Twist*, the prison chapters here read almost like a reply to the superficiality of Fagin's death scene. If prison is only the temporary detention of the innocent boy, who is sure to be saved in the end, or the horrible but just punishment of the thoroughly evil man, much of its terror disappears. But in *A Tale of Two Cities* it is a great deal more than this. Manette has been released from "105 North Tower," the royalist prison, and is living in the house of the revolutionary plotter, Defarge. He is free, but his freedom means nothing to him. He is always alone, and can scarcely bear visitors. He requires to be locked in his room, "because he has lived so long locked up, that he would be frightened—rave, tear himself to pieces—die—come to I know not what harm, if his door was left open."

He has forgotten his name, but remembers perpetually the number of his prison room, and he still occupies himself with the manual work he did in prison. But worse, he has not only forgotten himself as a human being, he has been virtually forgotten by his benefactors. Defarge does not pity him as a kind of dead trophy or example to stir up revolutionary feeling. So influential is Defarge's view of him that it momentarily infects even Defarge's daughter.

"I am afraid of it."

"Of it? Of what?"

"I mean of him . . . of my father."

We miss the point if we read this merely as a description of callous perversity. On the contrary, when the prisoner is described by the author, he appears in much the same light. "He, and his old canvas frock, and his loose stockings, and all his poor tatters of clothes, had, in a long seclusion from direct light and air, faded down to such a dull uniformity of parchment-yellow, that it would have been hard to say which was which." Here is Dickens's ultimate in misery, a suffering that cannot be relieved, pitied or understood, that is not aware of itself, and to the question "I hope you care to be recalled to life?" can only answer "I can't say."

And to make us universalise the picture, and apply it to the suffering world in general, Dickens placed at the end of the chapter this image: "Beneath that arch of unmoved and eternal lights; some, so remote from this little earth that the learned tell us it is doubtful whether their rays have even yet discovered it, as a point in space where anything is suffered or done. . . ."

In this chapter, Dickens achieved something new. He used the image of the prison for a steady gaze, without self-pity or hysteria, at the general miseries of life. For although Manette can recover his wits and his human dignity, the prison is lurking within him, ready to regain control, when a new emotional crisis occurs. At the time of his daughter's marriage he goes back to his unconscious shoemaking. Perhaps this incident has a somewhat unreal and contrived air. But its importance in the author's development is nevertheless considerable. Dickens was, as we have seen, exceptionally aware of external objects; his imagination was extraordinarily literal; his psychological grasp, which was eventually to become formidable, was slow to develop. His natural tendency, therefore, was to blame all the misery he observed on circumstances, on tyrants, on social conditions. So it was bound to take time for him to comprehend that the prison he was endlessly seeking to describe and understand was, in part, the mental creation of the prisoner, that to strike away the chains and fetters could not solve all the prisoner's problems. Having now realised this, having arrived at his own version of the discovery:

> "O the mind, mind has mountains; cliffs of fall
> Frightful, sheer, no-man fathomed."

he was eventually able to develop it in the case of Miss Havisham into a deep psychological study.

But it may be objected that all this special pleading does not improve the quality of the actual scene in which Manette returns to his shoemaking, if, as I have suggested, that is deficient. . . .

The consequences of Manette's hopeless misery are very instructive. When the Revolution comes, his long years of imprisonment under the old régime entitle Manette to a privileged position. He can use his influence on behalf of his accused son-in-law; and he can even say, "It all tended to a good end, my friend; it was not mere waste and ruin." When these hopes seem to be fulfilled, he is a proud and happy man. But the release of Evremonde is only temporary. He is once again denounced and sentenced to death. The melodramatic ending in which Evremonde is saved by the substitution of Carton, cannot obscure the significance of this. For Evremonde's second condemnation is occasioned by the reading of a document written by Manette in prison. The supposed utility of those long years in prison ends in disillusionment. And at this point, with sombre appropriateness, Manette returns, as Dorrit had done so much more convincingly, to the imbecile mode of consciousness which possessed him in his prison years.

So the direct and tangible value of prisoners' suffering is implicitly denied. But there is still a strange dignity in the prison, which comes to Evremonde as a surprise:

> In the instinctive association of prisoners with shameful crimes and disgrace, the newcomer recoiled from his company. But the crowning unreality of his long unreal ride, was, their all at once rising to receive him, with every refinement of manner known to the time, and with all the engaging graces and courtesies of life.

No doubt Dickens had read of some such scene in the French Revolution, but all the same, this dignity had personal significance also for him. It reduces the prison to a terror of manageable proportions. If it cannot be called a complete moral or artistic answer to the problem of the prison which he carried with him through his writing life, it at least contains no cheat or deception. . . .

## THE UNDERLYING EXPERIENCE
## OF PRISON IN *GREAT EXPECTATIONS*

In its treatment of prisons as in other ways too, *Great Expectations,* perhaps the most subtle and elusive of Dickens's books, is hard to classify. In the first place we have another, a more Gothic, more memorable, more sympathetic version, of the self-imposed imprisonment of Mrs. Clennam [in *Little Dorrit*].

> I saw that the bride within the bridal dress had withered like the dress, and like the flowers, and had no brightness left but the brightness of her sunken eyes. I saw that the dress had been put upon the rounded figure of a young woman, and that the figure upon which it now hung loose, had shrunk to skin and bone. Once, I had been taken to some ghastly waxworks at the Fair, representing I know not what impossible personage lying in state. Once, I had been taken to one of our old marsh churches to see a skeleton in the ashes of a rich dress, that had been dug out of a vault under the church pavement. Now waxwork and skeleton seemed to have dark eyes that moved and looked at me.

Unlike Mrs. Clennam and Mr. Dorrit and nearly all Dickens's other prisoners she is primarily someone who is seen. Her own mode of consciousness remains largely obscure. The word "waxwork" is significant, and it recurs in another context.

> While I looked about me here [Newgate prison], an exceedingly dirty and partially drunk minister of justice asked me if I would like to step in and hear a trial or so; informing me that he could give me a front place for half-a-crown, whence I should command a full view of the Lord Chief Justice in his wig and robes—mentioning that awful personage like waxwork, and presently offering him at the reduced price of eighteenpence.

What do these two passages have in common? In each case Pip imagines he is a detached spectator, that he can treat a new aspect of life as if it were a waxwork show. In each case he is really about to be deeply involved. And this is perhaps the key to the treatment of the prison in *Great Ex-*

*pectations*. It is no longer a dominant image casting long shadows on every part of the book. It is a fertile soil out of which things grow for the delight or the profit or the undoing of people who have never thought about this soil. A convict is the author of Pip's good fortune, but Pip will be horrified when he knows this. The incident in chapter eighteen (an improbable one if taken literally), of Pip travelling in the stage coach with the convicts, is no doubt meant to suggest the idea "All in the same boat." In *Little Dorrit* you could escape the prison but not forget it. Here you can ignore it but you cannot escape it. All Pip's wealth comes from the convict, and so does Estella. The satire upon Pip's genteel shame and horror are like Dickens's delayed self-punishment for his own. The situation is only made more intolerable by the fact that the convict for all his vulgar dreams of gentlemanliness, is lovable. Pip painfully helps him to escape—he gives him the help which Dickens perhaps failed to give his own father.

> I consumed the whole time in thinking how strange it was that I should be encompassed by all this taint of prison and crime; that in my childhood out on our lonely marshes on a winter evening I should have first encountered it; that, it should have reappeared on two occasions, starting out like a stain that was faded but not gone; that it should in this new way pervade my fortune and advancement.

In these words of Pip, Dickens expressed one of the great enigmas of his own life, one which it took him many years to comprehend. And, he expressed it here, perhaps for the first time clearly and simply, without elaboration or distortion. In such a case the simplest and clearest statement was the most difficult of all to achieve.

## THE RANGE AND COMPLEXITY OF PRISON EXPERIENCE IN DICKENS'S WORKS

It is difficult to sum up in a matter of such complexity. From one point of view Dickens's prolonged attack upon the subject may be seen as a struggle to find value, even usefulness in the prison experience. First melodramatically, as in *Oliver Twist*, and then more seriously in the case of Blandois in *Little Dorrit*, the prison is useful because it is necessary for the protection of society, and the restraint of wickedness. But Dickens really knew very well that this idea, whether true or not, was not the solution he was searching for. For one thing, it could not explain why the subject gripped his imagination. Then he tried to think of the suffering and confinement of prisoners as positively beneficial in their future lives. This concept seems for a time to govern the plot of *A Tale of Two Cities*. Manette's imprisonment apparently gives him the right, under a new revolutionary régime, to prevent the persecution of those he loves.

But one of the reasons why Dickens, even when not at his best, is such an interesting writer, is that his plots have a life of their own. There are frequent conflicts between the rational planning mind of the artist and a kind of hidden subconscious logic possessed by the story itself. Perhaps as the result of some such conflict, Manette's power to influence events proves to be an illusion; this signifies the impossibility, at this stage, of believing that the prison will be the cause of happiness.

But in the universal prisons of *Little Dorrit* and *Great Expectations,* we seem to detect in the author a despairing satisfaction in the idea that the prison is everywhere, is unavoidable, and is, like life itself, an inextricable mixture of pleasure and pain. It would seem that the prison became for Dickens emblematic of the whole problem of suffering. The man was so practical that he had to struggle to solve this problem in terms of necessary sacrifice for future progress and happiness in life. With one part of his mind at least, he approached the prison in a matter-of-fact, almost hedonistic vein. Such an attempt must fail. And so Dickens has really nothing to tell us about how to live in prison. . . .

But what he did, he did superbly. He presented an immense range of prison experience. He showed its intimate connection at every point with the lives of the free and respectable. He showed the relevance of the idea to many aspects of society, from the Bastille to the slums. He transformed personal shame and fear into art.

# Dickens's Crusade for Children

Arthur A. Adrian

Arthur A. Adrian analyzes the most deplorable conditions endured by Victorian children and shows how Dickens's novels take up the cause for their better treatment. Adrian relates the abuses—harsh discipline, work exploitation, neglect—to Dickens's own childhood suffering, and he explains how Dickens exaggerates his attacks on Victorian parents and society in his sympathy for all lonely, misunderstood, and abused children. Arthur A. Adrian began his career teaching in a rural school in Kansas and later taught at the University of Kansas, the University of Oregon, and Case-Western Reserve University in Ohio. He is the author of *Georgina Hogarth and the Dickens Circle* and many articles published in scholarly journals.

"In the little world in which children have their existence, whosoever brings them up, there is nothing so finely perceived and so finely felt, as injustice," observes Pip on the way his sadistic sister has brought him up "by hand" (*Great Expectations*). Subjected to periodic thumping, repeatedly put on a "mortifying and penitential" diet of bread crumbs and watered milk, and dismissed by adults as "naterally vicious," he has endured "perpetual conflict with injustice."

With this portrayal of Pip's boyhood Dickens was continuing into his final decade his crusade against the abuses inflicted on Victorian children. Identifying his own early suffering with theirs, he lashed out against a harsh society that victimized defenseless youngsters. From observation he knew only too well that many parents, regardless of their social status, repressed their children, denying them their individuality and their rights.

## RELIGIOUS JUSTIFICATION FOR SEVERE DISCIPLINE

Especially stern was the discipline in Dissenting and Evangelical families, whose "gloomy theology," like that of the Murdstones, "made all children to be a swarm of little vipers" (*David Copperfield*). Puritan by tradition and zealously reinforced by the Wesleyans, such discipline was based on the belief in original sin. Considered innately depraved, for they had been conceived in sin, children must be subdued into complete submission; and parents, acting in God's place, should instruct them to be truthful, obedient, punctual, and respectful toward their elders. Dire threats and frequent corporal punishment were thought necessary to curb natural depravity. The mildest measures consisted of sending the culprit to bed with blinds drawn, taking away his toys, putting him on a diet of bread and water, or standing him in a corner with face to the wall. If these measures failed, cuffings and floggings usually produced the desired result. On occasion they also produced physical injury, such as deafness from repeated ear boxing. That disobedience, lying, or even loss of temper led to eternal damnation was impressed on tender minds by memory gems like the following from *The Peep of Day:*

> Satan is glad when I am bad
> And hopes that I with him shall lie
> In fire and chains and dreadful pains.

"Take some time to speak a little to your children ... about their miserable condition by nature," James Hannay advises parents in *A Token for Children.* "They are not too little to die, nor too little to go to hell." Charles Kingsley was to show how such instruction could do irreparable damage to a child. In his *Alton Locke* the young Alton is never free of a guilty terror that he will wake one "morning in everlasting flames." But to the young John Ruskin[1] the thought of these flames was even more terrifying, more real, for his zealous Evangelical mother once held his baby finger over a burning candle because he had been untruthful. The pain, she told him, was a mere foretaste of what liars must endure in eternal hell.

Less sensational but not less damaging were the tortures inflicted on children by meaningless religious instruction.

---

1. British essayist

Catechized until they could parrot the doctrine of original sin and redemption, all beyond their comprehension, they grasped neither the New Testament message nor Christian ethics. Strict observance of the Sabbath, moreover, caused them to view the church as a place of sourness and gloom. Such was the chapel Arthur Clennam was marched off to three times on Sunday, "morally handcuffed" like a "military deserter" (*Little Dorrit*). . . .

## CHILDHOOD GUILT AND SUBMISSION

The sensitive child in such a narrowly religious home suffered guilt and shame. Like Pip he felt himself a sinner by the very fact of his birth. Such also would have been David Copperfield's fate, moreover, had he remained under the Murdstones' tutelage. Healthy ego thus diminished, many a child became unnaturally docile, subdued by the popular admonition, "Children, obey your parents in the Lord," for indeed obedience to parents was identical with obedience to God. . . .

Common platitudes of the time, such as "Break a child's will or he will break you" and "spare the rod and spoil the child," reflected the attitude toward youthful independence. "The first signs of self-will must be carefully looked for, plucked out by the roots before they [have] time to grow," warns Theobald Pontifex [a stern moralist]. There could be no relaxation of authority nor any undue show of tenderness. With characteristic and grimly humorous exaggeration, Dickens jabs at such harshness by having Susan Nipper, the otherwise good-natured young woman who watches over Florence Dombey, hold "that childhood like money, must be shaken and rattled and jostled about a good deal to keep it bright" (*Dombey and Son*). . . .

Regarded as little adults, children enjoyed no coddling. Even in prosperous homes life could be spartan. Only the physically fit child survived, as physicians were called in for none but extreme cases. For mere constitutional delicacy a rigorous hardening process was preferred. Augustus Hare (*The Years with Mother*) tells how his Aunt Esther attempted to "subdue him" because of the chilblains which left open wounds on his hands and feet. Her remedial program required him to sleep on a straw pallet under a coarse blanket, in an uncarpeted and unheated room. . . .

As for the child's intellect and imagination, they found little stimulation in such recommended juvenile literature as

Mrs. Barbauld's *Evenings at Home* and *Hymns in Prose*. As for Thomas Day's *Sandford and Merton,* any perceptive young reader would have seen it as a too obvious attempt to improve his morals. Of all the didactic and moralistic books, however, none strove more blatantly to promote virtue than Mrs. Sherwood's *History of the Fairchild Family*. The children of this model family endure endless sermonizing; they meditate in dark closets on their minor transgressions; they view a corpse on the gallows in order to ponder the wages of sin at first hand. . . .

### NEGLECT AMONG THE LOWER CLASSES

If in their zeal to perform their duty such middle-class parents as the Fairchilds lacked all empathy with their children, parents in the lowest class of all, the London underworld, lacked all concept of responsibility toward their offspring. Themselves born into a world of dirt, vermin, hunger, disease, and crime, they could only pass on their heritage. Consequently children, legitimate or not, were abandoned by their mothers in workhouses and deserted by roving fathers seeking employment. Their origin unknown, they had neither family nor home. Dickens summed it up when he wrote of Miss Wade: "Put her in a room in London here with any six people old enough to be her parents, and her parents may be there for anything she knows" (*Little Dorrit*). Roaming singly or in packs like young wolves, such abandoned vagrants became street Arabs, covered with rags, sheltering in arcades or empty cellars, huddled together for warmth, devouring spoiled fruit and vegetables thrown out of Covent Garden Market, begging, stealing, lying, cursing, plundering. The struggle to survive having made them destructive, brutish, cruel, they were hopeless outcasts, forced to keep moving. Of them William Blanchard Jerrold wrote in "Anybody's Child" (from *Household Words,* 4 February 1854): "Anybody's Child is a little fiend, a social curse, a hypocrite, a liar, a thief."

And in *The Haunted Man,* his last Christmas book, Dickens painted a poignant portrait of this "little fiend": "A face rounded and smoothed by some half-dozen years, but pinched and twisted by the experience of life. Bright eyes, but not youthful. Naked feet, beautiful in their childish delicacy,— ugly in blood and dirt that cracked upon them. A baby savage, a young monster, a child who had never been a child, a creature who might live to take the outward form of a man, but who, within, would live and perish a mere beast." . . . In *Our Mutual Friend,* his last completed novel, he still used irony to slash at society's neglect. "Show her a Christening," he comments on Pleasant Riderhood, the river scavenger's daughter, "and she saw a little heathen personage having quite a superfluous name bestowed upon it, inasmuch as it would be commonly addressed by some abusive epithet; which little personage was not in the least wanted by anybody, and would be shoved and banged out of everybody's way, until it should grow big enough to shove and bang."

Many such owners of "superfluous" names, if they survived the hazard of childhood, went to prison, were trans-

---

**DICKENS'S ACQUAINTANCE WITH JUVENILE CRIME AND ITS PUNISHMENT**

*In* Great Expectations, *Jaggers explains in detail why he rescued Estella. The passage indicates that Dickens was well acquainted with the treatment and punishment of children.*

"Now, Pip," said Mr. Jaggers, "put this case. Put the case that a woman, under such circumstances as you have mentioned, held her child concealed, and was obliged to communicate the fact to her legal adviser, on his representing to her that he must know, with an eye to the latitude of his defence, how the fact stood about that child. Put the case that at the same time he held a trust to find a child for an eccentric rich lady to adopt and bring up."

"I follow you, sir."

"Put the case that he lived in an atmosphere of evil, and that all he saw of children was, their being generated in great numbers for certain destruction. Put the case that he often saw children solemnly tried at a criminal bar, where they were held up to be seen; put the case that he habitually knew of their being imprisoned, whipped, transported, neglected, cast out, qualified in all ways for the hangman, and growing up to be hanged. Put the case that pretty nigh all the children he saw in his daily business life, he had reason to look upon as so much spawn, to develop into the fish that were to come to his net—to be prosecuted, defended, forsworn, made orphans, bedevilled somehow."

"I follow you, sir."

"Put the case, Pip, that here was one pretty little child out of the heap who could be saved."

ported, or, if cunning enough to elude the law, persisted in crime and debauchery. In Henry Mayhew's *London Labour and the London Poor* a statistical study of 150 juvenile thieves shows that nearly half had been in prison before, many more than once, six at least twenty-four times. And some of the offenders were only eight years old! "They have been either untaught, mistaught, maltreated, neglected, regularly trained in vice, or fairly turned into the streets to shift for themselves.... The censure then," Mayhew argues, "is attributable to parents, or to those who fill the place of parents—the state, or society." But as the records of the period confirm all too clearly, the state, having shirked its responsibilities, dealt sternly with children when they became public offenders. Brutal floggings of imprisoned juveniles, even capital punishment, were not uncommon. The Crown Calendar for the Lincolnshire Lent Assizes, 1818, records, for example, that fifteen-year-old George Crow, charged "on suspicion" of having stolen three pounds and sixpence, was sentenced to death....

In this vicious environment parents not uncommonly exploited their own children, sending them into the streets to beg and steal, selling their clothes for drink, even encouraging elder daughters to take up prostitution and then living on their earnings. Promiscuity was common among the laboring poor, for many spurned the institution of marriage. With a succession of men using her home as a temporary residence, a mother might have children sired by different fathers. A typical incident is recounted by a contemporary sociologist. A small boy, appearing in school with a new pair of boots, was asked where he had got them. "One of my fathers give 'em to me, mistress," he answered, "the one that's at home this week."

## CHILDREN EXPLOITED FOR WORK

When minor children could not be cared for at home, the parish had the right to apprentice them to any trade. Here industry abused them, sending them off to any part of the country, often to the cotton mills for forced labor. Mere babes of six and seven worked as long as twelve hours daily, in stifling lint-filled rooms, always in danger of being mangled by unfenced machinery. Barely able to get back to the dormitories after a long day, they crawled into beds left still warm by the last shift, their only cover a rough horse blanket. Should the mill fail and have to close, the children were set adrift to roam the countryside and beg for food. Toward such inhumanity the world took the callous attitude typified by the following comment in the House of Commons: "It would be highly injurious to the public to put a stop to the binding of so many apprentices to the cotton manufacturers, as it must necessarily raise the price of labour and enhance the price of cotton goods."

Even worse was the oppression of the chimney sweeps. Orphans, bastards, and unwanted stepsons, they were generally sold to, or kidnapped by, a master sweep, who worked them many hours and spent little on their keep. There was no schedule of regular meals; the boys bolted down their food whenever they could find time; at night they slept on bags of soot in some damp cellar. Small for their age, they were driven up narrow flues, where they sometimes got stuck in the crook of a chimney. In such emergencies their masters would try to bring them down by building a fire under them. . . .

Of all child labor, that in the coal mine was the most appalling. As early as age eight or nine, sometimes even at four or six, boys and girls were harnessed to little trucks of coal which they drew in a crouching position through low passages to the larger openings. It is hardly necessary to point out that the mortality rate of such children was high. Almost totally deprived of fresh air and sunshine, unable to cleanse themselves of the coal dust embedded in their scalps and skin, they built no resistance to disease. . . .

To be sure, by prohibiting the employment of children under nine in cotton mills, by reducing the hours and improving the working conditions of others, and by making some provision for holidays and education, the Factory Act of 1833 was designed to correct abuses. Still, although working children were to benefit from this and subsequent legislation, factory inspection was often lax and laws were not strictly enforced. Generally an apathetic public ignored the plight of the little drudges whose cheap labor helped to ensure England's place as the world's wealthiest nation.

## DICKENS'S CAMPAIGN ON BEHALF OF CHILDREN

In all fairness it must be pointed out that the preceding summary of child oppression is based partly on highly selective literature, such as novels, autobiographies of sensitive artists, and studies of certain slum areas. It should not be concluded, therefore, that all children in the nineteenth century were oppressed or physically abused, for many parents enjoyed a happy relationship with their families. And even in homes where austerity and strict discipline had been the rule, some of the children later recalled their upbringing without bitterness, grateful for the training that had prepared them for the responsibilities of adulthood. Still, because Dickens saw even isolated instances of childhood abuse as intolerable and often, to arouse public indignation, exaggerated them in his attacks, they must be considered here as a basis for his condemnation of Victorian parents and society in general. . . .

Dickens was concerned not only with families of the poor; his sympathies went out to children everywhere—to the lonely, the misunderstood, the mistreated, who were to be found in middle-class homes as well, where chilling piety masked selfish materialism. "I am the only child of parents who weighed, measured, and priced everything," reflects Arthur Clennam; "for whom what could not be weighed, measured, and priced, had no existence" (*Little Dorrit*). Whatever the social class, Dickens attributed childhood misery to "neglectful and unnatural parents," for whom he recommended "severe punishment" (*Household Words*, 5 April 1851). Indeed, he seems to have covered parents in general with the blanket of his disapproval, for as early as 1844 he declared that he had observed them to be "invariably" selfish in their relations with their children.

In his continuing crusade for the rights of children Dickens followed a tradition directly opposed to the Puritan and Wesleyan view of the child as inherently depraved. He upheld the cult of innocence, which stressed primeval goodness and natural piety. Deriving its inspiration from Rousseau,[2] it was continued by William Blake and William Wordsworth,[3] who saw children as seers, spiritually wiser than adults. . . . Dickens would use one of his earliest novels to portray childish purity and inherent wisdom triumphing over worldly evil.

Pondering the injustices inflicted upon defenseless children, Dickens kept returning to his traumatic boyhood. Memories of that period fired his indignation against par-

2. French philosopher Jean-Jacques   3. British poets

ents (and a society charged with parental responsibility) who either abandoned their children or exploited them for personal gain. In *The Haunted Man* he turned one of his fiercest attacks on those who tolerated such abuses: "There is not a father by whose side in his daily or nightly walk, these creatures walk; there is not a mother among all the ranks of loving mothers in this land; there is no one risen from the state of childhood, but shall be responsible in his or her degree for their enormity. There is not a country throughout the earth on which it would not bring a curse. There is no religion upon earth that it would not deny; there is no people upon earth it would not put to shame."

Spurred by poignant memories of his own childhood, Dickens used his art to launch a crusade that occupied him throughout his career. Though he was never to recover completely from the deep psychological wounds of his boyhood, he came to terms with his past by drawing upon memories of his own suffering for his efforts to reform the lot of nineteenth-century children. No subject so dominated his emotions, his thoughts, his utterances—epistolary, journalistic, or literary. For the genesis of his lifelong interest in parent-child relations it is necessary to consider the formative years of his boyhood.

# The Transforming World in Dickens's Novels

J. Hillis Miller

J. Hillis Miller argues that Dickens's heroes progress from confused, isolated individuals to free human spirits. Miller explains that the transformation occurs in stages as heroes search through adventure, love, divine Providence, and self-reliance. He cites heroes in the last novels who withdraw and then return to an imperfect world; after their temporary retreat, they have found their identity and can focus on the future. J. Hillis Miller has taught English at Johns Hopkins University and the University of California at Irvine. He is the author of *Charles Dickens: The World of His Novels*, *The Disappearance of God*, and *Poets of Reality*.

Certain elements persist through [Dickens's] work. Among the most important of these are the general situation of the protagonist at the beginning of the story and the general nature of the world he lives in. Each protagonist confronts, from moment to moment, a certain kind of world, a world in which inanimate objects, space and time, other people, and his own inner life have certain given modes of existence. These entities are initially, in most cases, distant from the protagonist, inimical, without comprehensible relation to him. The nonhuman world seems menacing and apparently has a secret life of its own, unfriendly to man, while the social world is an inexplicable game or ritual, in which people solemnly enact their parts in an absurd drama governed by mysterious conventions. Each Dickensian hero, then, lives like Paul Dombey, "with an aching void in his young heart, and all outside so cold, and bare, and strange" (*Dombey and Sons*). He is even alienated from himself, and views his own consciousness as something mysterious and separated from himself.

## ADVENTURES OF AN ALIENATED HERO

Beginning in isolation, each protagonist moves through successive adventures. . . . These adventures are essentially attempts to understand the world, to integrate himself in it, and by that integration to find a real self. In this interchange between mind and world there is in Dickens' characters and in the novels themselves as wholes a constant attempt to reach something transcendent, something more real than one's own consciousness or than the too solid everyday material world.

This supra-reality is perhaps caught in fleeting glimpses at the horizon of the material world, or in the depths beneath the upper layers of consciousness. In those depths are the regions of dreams, or of that hallucinated vision of things and people which is so characteristic of Dickens. The realm of images, where self is given a material form, and where things are transmuted into emblems of the self, is the very domain where the reality beyond or within reality may be momentarily apprehended. To put self and the sensible world it possesses as image in touch with these depths would be to transfigure the self, thus to validate it.

Dickens' protagonists, initially creatures of poverty and indigence, are constantly in search of something outside the self, something other than the self, and even something other than human, something which will support and maintain the self without vaporizing and engulfing it. Dickens' novels, then, . . . form a whole, a unified totality. Within this whole a single problem, the search for viable identity, is stated and restated with increasing approximation to the hidden center, Dickens' deepest apprehension of the nature of the world and of the human condition within it.

Dickens' recognition of the indifference or positive evil of much of the world was obscured by the high spirits of *Pickwick Papers*, so that Oliver Twist is the first of Dickens' heroes to dramatize unequivocally the plight of the disinherited orphan, lost in a dark and alien world. Oliver is rescued and the novel given a happy ending by a resolution which is standard for dozens of Victorian novels: the secrets of the orphan's birth are discovered and he inherits a secure place in the world. Only the intensity with which Dickens imagines and shares Oliver's sufferings gives authenticity to this conventional plot. So powerful is Dickens' fear of suggesting that the alienated hero should take matters into his own hands that he accepts a denouement which emphasizes the infantile passivity of his hero. Oliver is willing to accept a definition of his identity which comes from the outside and from the past.

## DISTORTED CHARACTERS ISOLATED FROM ONE ANOTHER AND SOCIETY

The novels which follow *Oliver Twist* show that a sense of the grotesque idiosyncrasies of people, their incommensurability with one another, is a central element in Dickens' vision of the world. But this partial shift from the melodrama of *Oliver Twist* back to the comedy of *Pickwick Papers* does not alter the fact that the central characters of *Nicholas Nickleby*, *The Old Curiosity Shop*, and *Barnaby Rudge* are, like Oliver, isolated in an inimical world. Indeed, the vision of people as wholly unlike one another and locked in the distortions of personal eccentricities is one of Dickens' most powerful ways of dramatizing the theme of isolation, and the inexhaustible power to bring into existence large numbers of comic or melodramatic grotesques, each alive with his own peculiar intensity of life, is perhaps Dickens' most extraordinary talent as a novelist. Though *Nicholas Nickleby*, *The Old Curiosity Shop*, and *Barnaby Rudge*, like *Oliver Twist*, depend for their resolutions on the discovery of something coming from the past and from outside the hero's own action, there is increasing recognition, especially in *The Old Curiosity Shop*, that the only complete escape from the alien city is through death. The death of Nell near the graveyard of a country church reflects back on Oliver's retreat to a happy rural paradise and suggests that it was an evasion of Dickens' problem, not a real solution.

In *Martin Chuzzlewit* Dickens faces this problem more squarely by bringing his hero into the open arena of society, and by minimizing the help he can get from his parents, grandparents, or ancestors. Here one of Dickens' central themes is fully expressed: the impossibility of achieving other than a sham identity by dependence on a society which is a masquerade of imposture and disguised self-seeking. Dickens sees in *Martin Chuzzlewit* that the purely human, cut off from any contact with what is above or beyond it and setting itself up as an end in itself, is factitious.[1] Martin must learn to repudiate all selfishness and hypocrisy and depend on what is most real in human nature: its spontaneous feelings of affection or loving-kindness for others. But this idea is blurred by an ending which recalls in some ways that of *Oliver Twist.*

## IDENTITY THROUGH LOVE

*Dombey and Son* and *David Copperfield,* the novels which directly follow *Martin Chuzzlewit,* complete one of the most important transformations of Dickens' imaginative vision: a movement from dependence on the child-parent relation as an escape from isolation to a dependence on the more adult solution of romantic love. *Dombey and Son* is Dickens' first mature analysis of the child-parent relation. It shows that to know and possess one's parents can be as much a cause of suffering as to be a friendless orphan. But Florence Dombey achieves real happiness not through the change in her father's attitude, but through her love for Walter Gay and his love for her, just as the center of *David Copperfield,* Dickens' most intimately personal novel, is the relation of David to Agnes. However, the opposition in *David Copperfield* between the hero's private memory and the power of Providence as alternative sources of the world's coherence, like the image of the "wild waves" in *Dombey and Son,* anticipates a central issue of Dickens' later novels: the question of the relation between man and the divine transcendence.

## THE INDIVIDUAL AND THE DIVINE

*Bleak House,* the first of Dickens' novels whose real protagonist is an entire society, shows people imprisoned by forces descending from the past, rather than liberated by them, as was the case in *Oliver Twist.* The only escape from the smothering fog of the Court of Chancery is Esther Summerson's power to make order in her immediate surroundings through the self-sacrifice and devotion of love. But Esther derives this power from her direct relation, through prayer, to divine grace. Esther is the avenue through which God's goodness, otherwise transcendent, descends into the human world. *Bleak House,* then, marks another transmutation in the nature of Dickens' imaginative world. Instead of waiting

1. lacking authenticity; sham

passively for a satisfactory place in society to descend upon her from the mysteries of the past, Esther must "trust in nothing, but in Providence and her own efforts." She must change the world around her through her own independent action in the present. Esther's discovery of her origin is an ironic reversal of the similar discovery in *Oliver Twist*. It liberates her from having any false expectations of society, and forces her to assume full responsibility for her own life.

The novels which follow *Bleak House*, however, show that this assumption of responsibility and the abnegating love it presupposes may not be so simply attained as they were for Esther. Dickens' later novels see the world as more and more shadowed and enclosed by the self-generating cruelty, injustice, and imposture of mankind. *Little Dorrit*, Dickens' darkest novel, is also his most profound exploration of the theme of perfect human goodness. All levels of society are so imprisoned in their selfish delusions that only the mystery of divine goodness incarnate in the childlike form of Little Dorrit can be a liberating force. But even *Little Dorrit* ends with the happy marriage of its heroine, whereas *A Tale of Two Cities* affirms that the self-sacrifice of perfect love, in order to be efficacious, may need the full sacrifice of life itself. *Great Expectations* pursues even further this exploration of the ambiguities of love. While *Hard Times* attempts to reconcile in the symbol of the "horse-riding" an image of the good society and the direct relation of love, *Great Expectations*, perhaps Dickens' most satisfactory treatment of the theme of romantic love, sees an irreconcilable opposition between Pip's relation to society and the final form of his love for Estella. Pip must choose between his "great expectations" and Estella. Moreover love is no longer seen as wholly guiltless and pure. Pip's initial love for Estella is as ambiguous in motivation as his "great expectations" from society, and his final relation to her is the mutual responsibility for one another's lives of two fallible and fallen people. Dickens' later novels give increasing recognition to the devastating and even anarchic power of love.

## NEGATION OF AN IDEAL AND
## ACCEPTANCE OF AN IMPERFECT WORLD

Still another reversal in orientation was reserved for Dickens' very last novels. This final surprising change in the nature of Dickens' vision of the world brings him in some ways closer to twentieth-century attitudes and themes than he had ever been before. It makes *Our Mutual Friend* the novel by Dickens perhaps most interesting to a contemporary reader, and makes us sorry that he did not live to finish *The Mystery of Edwin Drood.* This last change is a double one. It is a new notion that the transcendent spiritual power glimpsed at the margins or in the depths of the material world is not really a positive support for human values, even for good ones, but is the negation and reduction to nothing of all the human world indiscriminately. And it is a belief, deriving from this new vision of transcendence, that the human condition, with all its sufferings and unreality, can in no way be completely escaped, as long as life lasts. The human world is itself the only real support for human values. There is only one world for man. Dickens' last heroes and heroines come back to life after a purifying descent into the dark waters of death, but they come back to assume just that situation which was their given one in society. The difference is that their contact with the negative transcendence has liberated them to a new attitude toward their situation, an attitude which recognizes that value radiates not from any thing or power outside the human, but outward from the human spirit itself.

These, then, are the chief stages of Dickens' development. However, the most important single change in Dickens' novels, and the true turning point of his imaginative development, is a reversal which corresponds to a fundamental transformation of attitude in his century. This change can be defined as the rejection of the past, the given, and the exterior as sources of selfhood, and a reorientation toward the future and toward the free human spirit itself as the only true sources of value. To affirm this is to recognize the otherness of the nonhuman world, and the fact that it does not in itself offer any support to the creation of a humanly significant world. Rather than receiving selfhood as a gift from the outside and from the past, man, in Dickens' last novels, imposes value on himself and on the world as he assumes his future, including his death, in a dynamic process of living. The terminal point of *Our Mutual Friend,* as of the work of Dickens as a whole, is man's reaffirmation, after a withdrawal, of his particular, limited, engagement in the world and in society. This engagement takes the form of an acceptance of intimate relations with other people, and of a concrete, forward-moving action, oriented toward the future. Such action manipulates and gives value to the world at the same time that it derives value and identity from the solidity of that world. A man can transform his situation by assuming it, and only thus can the self find an external support for its identity and reconcile at last freedom and substantiality. Only by living in the mode of present participles can the self have an authentic existence, that is, only by living in the mode of an immediate present which is becoming future, and in the mode of a verbal action which is in the very process of becoming substantial and real as it alters the world and identifies itself with it: "Bella was fast developing a perfect genius for home. All the loves and graces seemed (her husband thought) to have taken domestic service with her, and to help her to make home engaging. . . . Such weighing and mixing and chopping and grating, such dusting and washing and polishing, such snipping and weeding and trowelling and other small gardening, such making and mending and folding and airing, such diverse arrangements . . . !" (*Our Mutual Friend*).

It is only by "such diverse arrangements" of the world that Bella ceases to be the "doll in the doll's house" (the phrase gave Ibsen[2] a title and a theme). And it is only by such a perpetual dynamic interaction between self and world that all men, for Dickens, can escape from the dilemma of either having no identity, or having one imposed from the outside on its passive recipient. Each man, in this way, can give himself a life which is constantly renewing itself, constantly perpetuating itself. To take responsibility for arranging the world is to take responsibility for making the self, and to escape at last from the grim alternatives of guilty action, passivity, or isolation which are initially the sole possibilities in the imaginative universe of Dickens.

---

2. Norwegian playwright Henrik Ibsen influenced the development of modern drama with realistic plays such as *A Dolls House*.

# CHAPTER 2

# Entertaining Stories for Serial Publication

READINGS ON
CHARLES DICKENS

# Pickwick Papers Reflects Dickens's Developing Talents

Philip Hobsbaum

Philip Hobsbaum notes that the first half of *Pickwick Papers* barely relates to the second half and that no central theme unifies the novel. Its popularity derives from Dickens's skillful telling: the details depicting humorous characters and the exaggerated actions comprising the episodes, or set pieces. Most memorable, according to Hobsbaum, are the medical students' party and the trial of Bardell versus Pickwick. Philip Hobsbaum has taught at Queens University in Northern Ireland and the University of Glasgow in Scotland. He is the author of *Essentials of Literary Criticism, Tradition and Experiment in English Poetry,* and *A Reader's Guide to D.H. Lawrence.*

*Pickwick Papers* is an extraordinary example of a novel outgrowing its original conception. The very Pickwick Club that gives the book its name has a real existence in the first chapter only, as a satire on the newly founded British Association for the Advancement of Science. There is really no need for its formal dissolution in the last chapter of all.

The interest of the novel builds up very much with the development of Pickwick himself. At first he is one of a number of eccentrics who go careering round the countryside, and is only differentiated from his associates by being less given to a prevailing humour. But, with the introduction of Sam Weller, his stature increases—a demonstration that the central figure of a novel benefits greatly through being seen through the eyes of an ancillary character. It was not simply the appearance of Sam in the fourth number of *Pickwick* that caused the sales to go up, nor yet the superior quality of the engravings of 'Phiz'. Rather its increasing popularity was due to an all-round tightening and sharpening of the writing, and this could easily be demonstrated by a comparison between the quality of the prose in the earlier episodes with that in the later ones. Dickens had already given evidence of his command over cockney idiom in such sketches as 'Seven Dials' and 'The Omnibus Cad'; it goes with his understanding of cockney character. In Sam Weller he was able to concentrate this into a single figure, and to use it as a satirical commentary upon middle-class *moeurs*[1] thereafter.

## SAM WELLER SHOWCASES PICKWICK

Sam Weller is first introduced to us as a lower servant in a suburban inn. From the first he is sharply realized in 'a coarse-striped waistcoat, with black calico sleeves, and blue glass buttons'. And his speech has the same distinctness of quality. Almost his first remark, when requested to give priority to a particular guest's boots, is 'Ask number twenty-two vether he'll have them now, or vait' till he gets 'em'. His objection is a democratic one: he shines the shoes according to the time people have asked to be woken up in the morning. 'No, no,' he goes on, 'reg'lar rotation, as Jack Ketch said, ven he tied the men up'—Jack Ketch being the public hangman. And this sturdy independence, together with macabre undertones, is a characteristic of his speech throughout—unparaphrasable, as Dickens's first Russian translator was to find. These 'Wellerisms', as they came to be called, are very much a part of Sam's utterance on each appearance: 'Business first, pleasure afterwards, as King Richard the Third said ven he stabbed the other King in the Tower, afore he smothered the babbies'. The mode of utterance is at once comic and macabre, Sam is attractive and charming, as is shown by his success with the ladies, and physically formidable, as witness his combats with beadles, constables, and other emblems of authority. Altogether he becomes a symbol of the sturdy, independent workingman—'footman, groom, gamekeeper, seedsman, or a sort of compo of every one of 'em'.

But Sam Weller does not stand alone. Pickwick himself, once the early caricature episodes are over, emerges as a representative of a settled middle class—'retired, and of considerable independent property'. We must beg the question of how this was acquired. Pickwick shines as an example of

1. customs, habits, morals

what every good rich man should be: defiant to villains, courteous to ladies, understanding towards the young, magnanimous to his enemies. It is no accident that the novel is dedicated to Thomas Noon Talfourd, the kindly judge and amateur author who went out of his way to befriend young aspirants such as Dickens himself. Only in the earlier episodes does Pickwick act out a stupendous ignorance of the world—hotels, law-courts, politics—as though he had been born, full-grown, in 1827 or thereabouts, without any discernible past. It is near the beginning of the book, also, that he is found drunk in a wheelbarrow. But his character progressively develops; it is noticeable that his generous behaviour towards Jingle occurs near the end.

## JINGLE COUNTERS PICKWICK

This character, Jingle, is one of the elements designed to stiffen the plot. At first he is introduced as just another counter in the apparently random permutations of *Pickwick Papers*. But Dickens evidently saw his future possibilities as a trickster. From the first, like Sam Weller, he has a remarkable style of speech: proceeding in jerks, apparently by free association. Of Spain he remarks,

> Conquests! Thousands. Don Bolaro Fizzgig—Grandee—only daughter—Donna Christina—splendid creature—loved me to distraction—jealous father—high-souled daughter—handsome Englishman—Donna Christina in despair prussic acid stomach pump in my portmanteau—operation performed—old Bolaro in ecstacies—consent to our union—join hands and floods of tears—romantic story—very.

This utterance has some odd antecedents. We may reject suggestions that Jingle's disjointed phraseology derives from eccentric characters in Tobias Smollett or Theodore Hook.[2] Rather he would appear to have, like so many Dickensian figures, his origin in real life, or real life as presented in Dr Johnson's hastily written account of his travels in France: 'There we waited on the ladies to Monville's.—Captain Irwin with us.—Spain. County towns all beggars.—At Dijon he could not find the way to Orleans.—Cross roads of France very bad.—Five soldiers.—Woman.—Soldiers escaped.—The Colonel would not lose five men for the sake of one woman.—The magistrate cannot seize a soldier but by the Colonel's permission, etc., etc.' It is impossible to decide whether this is a tran-

2. British novelists before Dickens

script of the Captain's speech or simply Johnson's mode of recording impressions; certainly the rest of the narrative is similarly jerky. But, as it stands, it resembles the manner of Jingle more than any other prototype that has been suggested. This manner, like the more circumstantial mode of speech in the utterance of Sam Weller, affords ample opportunity for far-fetched anecdote; and such anecdote, in every sense of the word, is the life of both these characters.

And both, so to speak, give Pickwick his chance to live. If Sam acts as a perpetual protector to his master, then Jingle is an intermittent gadfly. He first elopes with a maiden aunt and has to be bought off; later he is found inveigling his way into the social circle of the Mayor of Ipswich. He is, after Weller, the second of the linchpins that support what continuous action *Pickwick* has.

## MRS BARDELL ACCUSES PICKWICK

The third is the breach of promise case centring on Mrs Bardell. This action is based on a kind of misunderstanding familiar in early Dickens. Mr Pickwick, in announcing his intention of hiring a manservant, is taken by his landlady to be making her a proposal of marriage. The main merit of this event is that it culminates in the comic set-piece of *Pickwick Papers,* the trial of Bardell v. Pickwick. Like a great deal else that seems far-fetched in Dickens, this is based upon a collocation of ascertainable facts, and on characters in real life. The judge in the case, Mr Justice Stareleigh, is all too close to his original, Sir Stephen Gazelee. Even more remarkable is the basis for the prosecuting attorney. The Serjeant Buzfuz of the case was based on a Serjeant Bompas— described by one of his contemporaries as stout, sandy, and forceful in his efforts to press his point upon a jury. The plot-material derived from a different but equally usable source: the celebrated Norton-Melbourne case, which Dickens himself had reported in twenty-six columns the month before he wrote his fictional version. Mr Norton had brought an action against the Prime Minister, Lord Melbourne, for 'criminal conversation' (namely, adultery) with his wife. The evidence was so trivial and the testimony so corrupt that the jury returned an acquittal without leaving the box. The prosecution in this case, as in that of Bardell v. Pickwick, cited incriminating letters: "'I will call about half past 4. Yours. Melbourne'" . . . The style and form of these notes, Gentlemen, seems to import much more than they contain. Cautiously, I admit, they are worded; there are no professions of love . . . but still they are not the letters of an ordinary acquaintance.' The colour and verve of the trial in *Pickwick* comes from Dickens's remarkable combination of the Melbourne facts with the Bompas manner:

> They are covert, sly, underhanded communications, but, fortunately, far more conclusive than if couched in the most glowing language and the most poetic imagery . . . 'Garraway's, twelve o'clock. Dear Mrs B.—Chops and Tomata sauce. Yours, Pickwick.' Gentlemen, what does this mean? Chops and Tomata sauce. Yours, Pickwick! Chops! gracious heaven! and Tomata sauce! Gentlemen, is the happiness of a sensitive and confiding female to be trifled away by such shallow artifices as these?

Needless to say, the jury finds against Pickwick, and his refusal to pay damages and costs lands him in a debtors' prison. This is by far the grimmest part of the book. Here, again, Dickens's early experiences—as distinct from his reading—come into play. Weeds like Mivens the Zephyr and Smangle the Rake flourish happily in the close atmosphere of the Fleet Prison; while the cobbler, ruined by his legacy, sleeps under a table to remind himself of the four-poster bed he will never be able to occupy again. Characters such as these have a satire and poignancy we shall look for in vain in Smollett. In this episode, though not in the rest of *Pickwick*, we have intimations of Dickens's later powers of symbolism. 'A birdcage, sir,' says Sam, 'Veels within veels, a prison in a prison.' Or 'a lean and haggard woman, too　a prisoner's wife—who was watering, with great solicitude, the wretched stump of a dried-up withered plant, which, it was plain to see, could never send forth a green leaf again;—too true an emblem, perhaps, of the office she had come there to discharge.' . . .

Dickens himself testified that, when he went to prison to see his parents, he was always keen to hear from his mother what she knew about the histories of the debtors in the place. It is clear both observation and narrative had deeply penetrated his youthful mind.

Curiously enough, both of Pickwick's adversaries, Jingle and Mrs Bardell, end up in this prison, and Pickwick has a chance to show his magnanimity by being the instrument of their release. It is here that the ghost-novel which runs throughout the apparently random episodes of *Pickwick* asserts itself, and shows us what could have been done with a sounder concept, a little forethought, and some resistance to an over-simple tradition. As it is, the second half is, at once, grimmer than the first and far more unified in action. . . .

## SHIFTS AND CHANGES IN *PICKWICK PAPERS*

Certainly the earlier part of *Pickwick Papers* has little to do with the remainder of the book. One feels embarrassed by the hobbledehoydom[3] of the manoeuvres at Chatham, the Rochester duel, and the Eatanswill election. Crude, also, is the device of the interpolated tales. Seven of the nine occur in the first half of the novel, where there is comparatively little plot and the character is that of miscellany. They succeed only in dissipating what sustained interest the action has. One cannot put them on the level of the anecdotes told by Jingle or by Sam Weller, for the characters that tell these tales exist only as mouthpieces. Nor is there any thematic connection: the juxtaposition of the Madman's Manuscript with the episode of Bill Stumps's mark serves only to establish the versatility of 'Boz'; and neither does much to show his genius. It may be that the tales in *Pickwick* were originally composed for independent publication, but were incorporated into the main enterprise when the latter showed itself to be far more profitable. . . .

Enough should have been said by now to establish that *Pickwick Papers* exists on a number of different levels, not all of them related. One is almost driven to conclude that the book is best read as a collection of short stories that happen to be about the same characters. Some of the best episodes, indeed, have little to do with what centrality of focus the book can boast. The splendid scene of the medical students' party, a set-piece for Dickens's future readings, ranks only a little below Bardell v. Pickwick. Its wealth of detail would bear a fair amount of examination: one thinks of George Orwell's remarks on the subject in his essay on Dickens in *Inside the Whale.* The whole scene turns on the perennial need of homeless young bachelors to live in the houses of people who are middle-aged and staid. The rent of these tenants is welcome, but it goes along with habits that are incompatible with the settled ways of their hosts. This particular episode is decked out with macabre anecdote and drunken squabble and still farther enriched by the inclusion of a landlady with

3. awkwardness, immaturity

unparalleled gifts of invective. Mr Pickwick is present, but merely as a spectator. Like so much else in *Pickwick Papers*, Bob Sawyer's party could very well stand as a sketch on its own. And the other appearances of Sawyer and his friends have similar virtues.

In the end, we do not care so much about Pickwick and his three friends gallivanting about the countryside. Rather it is the set-pieces of the Pickwick trial and the Sawyer party that have prior claim on our attention. Moreover, the shadowy lineaments of another novel, to do with the fall of pride and one man's compassion for another, assert themselves at certain turning-points of the total action. There is, after all, a grim side to this book; one which deals with imprisonment, poverty, the checks and blights of existence. No doubt *Pickwick Papers* is rightly considered the funniest of Dickens's novels. Yet what is most noticeable about this achievement of Dickens's youth is what leads on to the great work of his maturity: a feeling, between bouts of frenetic escapism, of claustrophobia; a sense, among all the oases of hospitality and benevolence, of the expanse of waste even in the most successful of lives.

# Fairy-Tale Form in
# *A Christmas Carol*

Harry Stone

Harry Stone argues that Dickens employs fairy-tale
elements in *A Christmas Carol*. According to Stone,
Dickens starts off with ghosts and spirits, which manipulate the action in a setting of animated weather,
buildings, and objects. Events and characters take on
symbolic qualities, especially Scrooge, the archetypal
stingy man. These fairy-tale elements allow Dickens
to make rapid shifts in time, to fuse several levels of
meaning, and to illustrate a timeless moral. Harry
Stone has taught English at Northwestern University
in Illinois and California State University at North-
ridge. He is the editor of a book compiling Dickens's
notes on his novels and author of *Dickens the Craftsman* and *Dickens' Centennial Essays.*

Dickens wrote five Christmas books: A *Christmas Carol*
(1843), *The Chimes* (1844), *The Cricket on the Hearth* (1845),
*The Battle of Life* (1846), and *The Haunted Man* (1848). . . .
The Christmas books draw their innermost energies from
fairy tales: they exploit fairy-tale themes, fairy-tale happenings, and fairy-tale techniques. Indeed the Christmas books
*are* fairy tales. As Dickens himself put it, he was here taking
old nursery tales and "giving them a higher form.". . .

The design could hardly be simpler or more direct. A protagonist who is mistaken or displays false values is forced,
through a series of extraordinary events, to see his errors.
This familiar, almost pedestrian given is interfused with
fairy-tale elements, a commingling that shapes and transfig-
ures every aspect of the design. Storybook signs set the
mood, herald the onset of the action, and enforce the moral
lessons. Magical happenings dominate the story. The crucial
action takes place in a dream or vision presided over by su-

Excerpted from Harry Stone, *Dickens and the Invisible World: Fairy Tales, Fantasy, and
Novel-Making* (Bloomington: Indiana University Press, 1979). Copyright ©1979 by
Harry Stone. Reprinted by permission of the author.

pernatural creatures who control what goes on. The resolution occurs when the happenings of the vision—a magically telescoped survey of the protagonist's life, and a masquelike representation of the consequences of his false attitudes—force him to reassess his views. In the fashion of most fairy stories, the moral is strongly reiterated at the end. . . .

[Dickens] could now show misery and horror and yet do so in a context of joyful affirmation. He could depict evil flourishing to its ultimate flowering and still deny that flowering. He could introduce the most disparate scenes, events, and visions without losing the reader's confidence. He could manipulate time with no need to obey the ordinary laws of chronology. He could make his characters and events real when he wished them real, magical when he wished them magical. He could effect overnight conversions which could be justified aesthetically. He could teach by parable rather than exhortation. And he could deal with life in terms of a storybook logic that underscored both the real and the ideal. . . .

## SETTING THE SCENE

In *A Christmas Carol,* to take the first of the Christmas books, Dickens adapts fairy-tale effects and fairy-tale techniques with marvelous skill. All readers are aware of the ghosts and spirits that manipulate the story, but these supernatural beings are only the most obvious signs of a pervasive indebtedness to fairy stories. Dickens himself emphasized that indebtedness. He subtitled his novelette *A Ghost Story of Christmas,* and he followed this spectral overture with other magical associations. In the preface to the *Carol* he told potential readers that he had endeavored "in this ghostly little book, to raise the Ghost of an Idea." Then he went on: "May it haunt their houses pleasantly and no one wish to lay it!" The chapter headings continue this emphasis. Four of the five headings reinforce supernatural expectations: "Marley's Ghost," "The First of the Three Spirits," "The Second of the Three Spirits," and "The Last of the Spirits." With such signposts at the outset, we can expect the journey itself to be full of wondrous events. We are not disappointed, though the opening begins disarmingly enough. It insists on the deadness of Marley and then drifts into a long, facetious reference to the ghost of Hamlet's father. The narrator's attitude is worldly and commonsensical, but Marley's deadness and the ghost of Hamlet's father set the scene for the wild events that are about to take place.

Scrooge sets the scene too. He has much of the archetypal miser in him, but he is more of an ordinary man than his immediate prototypes, prototypes such as Gabriel Grub, Arthur Gride, Ralph Nickleby, and Jonas Chuzzlewit.[1] Yet at the same time Scrooge is compassed round with supernatural attributes that cunningly suffuse his fundamental realism. One soon sees how this process works. The freezing cold that pervades his inner being frosts all his external features and outward mannerisms (nipped and pointed nose, shrivelled cheek, stiffened gait, red eyes, blue lips, grating voice), and this glacial iciness chills all the world without. "He carried his own low temperature always about with him; he iced his office in the dog-days; and didn't thaw it one degree at Christmas. . . . No warmth could warm, no wintry weather chill him." In this respect Scrooge is a prototype of Mr. Dombey. That cold gentleman freezes and congeals his small universe with haughty frostiness.

## STORYBOOK MAGIC

The story proper of *A Christmas Carol* begins with the traditional "Once upon a time." After this evocative opening Dickens quickly intensifies the storybook atmosphere. Scrooge lives in Marley's old chambers, and Marley died seven years ago on Christmas Eve, that is, seven years ago on the night the story opens. It is a foggy night. Nearby houses dwindle mysteriously into "mere phantoms"; ghostly forms loom dimly in the hazy mist. Out of such details, out of cold, fog, and frost, and out of brief touches of contrasting warmth, Dickens builds an atmosphere dense with personification, animism, anthropomorphism, and the like. The inanimate world is alive and active; every structure, every object plays its percipient role in the unfolding drama. Buildings and gateways, bedposts and door knockers become sentient beings that conspire in a universal morality. Everything is connected by magical means to everything else. Scrooge's chambers are a case in point. The narrator tells us that they are in a lonely, isolated building that must have played hide-and-seek with other houses in its youth, run into a yard where it had no business to be, forgotten its way out again, and remained there ever since. This lost, iso-

1. characters in Dickens's other books

lated, cutoff building, fit residence for a lost, isolated, cutoff man, has its own special weather and tutelary spirit. The fog and frost hang so heavy about the black old gateway of this building "that it seemed as if the Genius of the Weather sat in mournful meditation on the threshold."

Given a universe so magical and responsive, we are hardly surprised when Scrooge momentarily sees Marley's face glowing faintly in his front-door knocker, its "ghostly spectacles turned up on its ghostly forehead." When Scrooge sees an equally ghostly hearse on his staircase a few moments later, we know that he is in for a night of it. Thus we are fully prepared for Marley's ghost when it does appear, and we know how to interpret its every movement and accoutrement. Marley's ghost is a superb compound of social symbolism, wild imagination, realistic detail, and grisly humor. It moves in its own strange atmosphere, its hair and clothes stirring curiously, as though agitated by "the hot vapour from an oven"; it wears a bandage round its head, and when it removes this death cloth, its lower jaw drops down upon its breast. Like Blake's city-pent Londoner, Marley's ghost drags and clanks its "mind-forg'd manacles," the chain it "forged in life" and girded on of its "own free will"; like the ghost of Hamlet's father, it is doomed to walk the night and wander restlessly abroad. Scrooge is skeptical of this apparition, but he is no match for the ghost's supernatural power. Like the Ancient Mariner with the wedding guest, the ghost "hath his will." When Scrooge offers his last resistance, the ghost raises a frightful cry, shakes its chains appallingly, and takes the bandage from round its head. Scrooge falls on his knees and submits. Like the wedding guest, now Scrooge "cannot choose but hear." And as in the *Ancient Mariner,* where the wedding guest's struggle and reluctant submission help us suspend our disbelief, in *A Christmas Carol* Scrooge's struggle and submission help us to a like suspension. The ghost has accomplished its mission; the work of the three spirits, work that will culminate in Scrooge's redemption (and our enlightenment), can now begin.

### THE GHOSTS AS ALLEGORICAL FIGURES AND SUPERNATURAL AGENTS

The three spirits or ghosts (Dickens uses the terms interchangeably) are allegorical figures as well as supernatural agents. The Ghost of Christmas Past combines in his person and in his actions distance and closeness, childhood and age, forgetfulness and memory; in a similar fashion the Ghost of Christmas Present is a figure of ease, plenty, and joy—an embodiment of the meaning of Christmas; the Ghost of Christmas Yet to Come, on the other hand, a hooded and shrouded Death, bears implacable witness to the fatal course Scrooge has been pursuing. Each spirit, in other words, enacts a role and presides over scenes that befit its representation. But it is the scenes rather than the spirits that are all-important. The scenes embody Dickens's message in swift vignettes and unforgettable paradigms—Fezziwig's ball, the Cratchits' Christmas dinner, Scrooge's lonely grave. By means of the fairy-tale machinery Dickens can move instantaneously from magic-lantern picture to magic-lantern picture, juxtaposing, contrasting, commenting, and counterpointing, and he can do all this with absolute freedom and ease. He can evoke the crucial image, limn the archetypal scene, concentrate on the traumatic spot of time, with no need to sketch the valleys in between. Like Le Sage much earlier in *The Devil upon Two Sticks* (a boyhood favorite of Dickens), he can fly over the unsuspecting city, lift its imperturbable rooftops, and reveal swift tableaus of pathos and passion; like Joyce much later in the opening pages of *A Portrait of the Artist as a Young Man,* he can race through the years, linger here and there, and provide brief glimpses of the unregarded moments that move and shape us. The overall effect, however, is more like that of a richly colored Japanese screen. Amid swirling mists and dense clouds one glimpses prototypical scenes of serenity and turmoil, joy and nightmare horror.

## TRUTH EMBODIED IN SCROOGE

Through Scrooge Dickens attempts to embody symbolic, social, psychological, and mythic truth. Scrooge is an outrageous miser and ogre, but he is also an emblem of more ordinary pathology: he is an epitome of all selfish and self-regarding men. In his latter aspect, he touches our lives. He allows us to see how self-interest—an impulse that motivates each one of us—can swell to monster proportions. He shows us how not to live, and then, at the end, he points us toward salvation. That lesson has social as well as symbolic ramifications. We are made to see that in grinding Bob Cratchit Scrooge grinds himself, that in letting Tiny Tim perish he perishes alive himself. All society is connected: individual actions are not self-contained and personal, they have social consequences; social evils are not limited and discrete, they taint the whole society. These ideas, of course, were not unique to Dickens. They were being preached by many Victorians, by two such different men—both friends of Dickens—as Douglas Jerrold and Thomas Carlyle,[2] for example. But Dickens presents these ideas in a more seductive guise than any of his contemporaries. And he blends teaching with much else.

For one thing, he merges symbolic paradigms and social doctrines with psychological analysis. By means of a few swift childhood vignettes he gives us some notion of why Scrooge became what he is. The first spirit shows Scrooge an image of his early self: "a solitary child, neglected by his friends," and left alone in school at Christmas time. This scene of loneliness and neglect is mitigated by a single relief: the boy's intense reading. The reading is not simply referred to, it comes to life, a bright pageant of color and warmth in his drab isolation. The exotic characters from that reading troop into the barren room and enact their familiar adventures. Scenes from *The Arabian Nights* flash before Scrooge, then images from *Valentine and Orson,* then vignettes from *The Arabian Nights* again, then episodes from *Robinson Crusoe*—all as of yore, all wonderfully thrilling and absorbing. Scrooge is beside himself with excitement. The long-forgotten memory of his lonely self and of his succoring reading softens him: he remembers what it was to be a child; he wishes that he had given something to the boy who sang a Christmas carol at his door the night before. A moment later Scrooge is looking at a somewhat older image of his former self, again alone in a school, again left behind at Christmas time. But now his sister Fan enters and tells him that he can come home at last, that father is kinder now and will permit him to return, that Scrooge is to be a man and "never to come back here" again. These memories also soften Scrooge.

The memories, of course, are versions of Dickens's own experiences: the lonely boy "reading as if for life," and saved by that reading; the abandoned child, left in Chatham to finish the Christmas term, while the family goes off to London;

2. Jerrold was a playwright and humorist; Carlyle an essayist and historian

the banished son (banished while Fanny remains free), exiled by his father to the blacking warehouse and then released by him at last. These wounding experiences, or rather the *Carol* version of them, help turn Scrooge (and here he is very different from the outward Dickens) into a lonely, isolated man intent on insulating himself from harm or hurt. In a subsequent vignette, a vignette between him and his fiancée, Scrooge chooses money over love. He is the victim of his earlier wound. He seeks through power and aggrandizement to gird himself against the vulnerability that had scarred his childhood. But in making himself invulnerable, he shuts out humanity as well. This happens to Scrooge because, paradoxically, in trying to triumph over his past, he has forgotten it; he has forgotten what it is to be a child, he has forgotten what it is to be lonely and friendless, to cry, laugh, imagine, yearn, and love. The first spirit, through memory, helps Scrooge recover his past, helps him recover the humanness (the responsiveness and fellow feeling) and the imagination (the reading and the visions) that were his birthright, that are every man's birthright.

## THE EFFECTIVENESS OF THE FAIRY-TALE FORMAT

All this, and much more, is done swiftly and economically with the aid of Dickens's fairy-tale format. The rapid shifts from scene to scene, the spirits' pointed questions and answers, the telescoping, blurring, and juxtaposition of time, the fusion of allegory, realism, psychology, and fancy—all are made possible, all are brought into order and believability, by Dickens's storybook atmosphere and storybook devices. *A Christmas Carol* has a greater unity of effect, a greater concentration of thematic purpose, a greater economy of means towards ends, and a greater sense of integration and cohesiveness than any previous work by Dickens.

*A Christmas Carol* is the finest of the Christmas books. This preeminence results from its consummate melding of the most archetypal losses, fears, and yearnings with the most lucid embodiment of such elements in characters and actions. No other Christmas book displays this perfect coming together of concept and vehicle. The result is a most powerful, almost mythic statement of widely held truths and aspirations. Scrooge represents every man who has hardened his heart, lost his ability to feel, separated himself from his fellow men, or sacrificed his life to ego, power, or accumulation. The symbolic force of Scrooge's conversion is allied to the relief we feel (since we are all Scrooges, in part) in knowing that we too can change and be reborn. This is why we are moved by the reborn Scrooge's childlike exultation in his prosaic physical surroundings, by his glee at still having time to give and share. We too can exult in "Golden sunlight; Heavenly sky; sweet fresh air; merry bells"; we too can cry, "Oh, glorious. Glorious!"; we too can give and share. Scrooge assures us that we can advance from the prison of self to the paradise of community. The *Carol*'s fairy-tale structure helps in that assurance. The structure evokes and objectifies the undefiled world of childhood and makes us feel that we, like Scrooge, can recapture it. Deep symbolic identifications such as these, identifications that stir us whether we are consciously aware of them or not, give *A Christmas Carol* its enduring grip on our culture. *A Christmas Carol* is a myth or fairy tale for our times, one that is still full of life and relevance. Its yearly resurrection in advertisement, cartoon, and television program, its reappearance in new versions (in Bergman's *Wild Strawberries,* to cite only one instance), testify to this.

# Dickens's Philosophy of Christmas

Louis Cazamian

Louis Cazamian calls Dickens's point of view in the Christmas stories a blend of Christianity and socialism that can be identified by four points: The birthday of Christ is a symbol of moral and social renewal; the poor have a duty to find hope and act with goodness; workers should not initiate socialistic reforms for more power and better wages; but the rich have a moral obligation to care for the poor. According to Cazamian, Dickens feels most hostile toward those who promote individualism. Louis Cazamian taught at the Sorbonne, University of Paris. In 1904 he considered Dickens and other authors in a pioneering work of historical criticism entitled *Le Roman Social en Angleterre* (*The Social Novel in England*).

What emerges if this tale [*The Chimes*] is put together with the other Christmas Stories, and with scattered passages in his work where Dickens defined his thought distinctly, is 'Christmas Philosophy'. It is a vague and sentimental form of Christian socialism. Bolder in making criticisms than in offering positive policies, it extols intervention in the name of religious idealism. Considered historically, it answers the needs of a society which had by then half-disappeared. It suits the personal relationships of the family business and the small workshop. In this sense it could be called reactionary, but from all other points of view, it is progressive. Dickens unreservedly disapproves of explicit manifestations of reactionary social attitudes. He refuses to let the need for benevolent authority tempt him into a desire for the political tutelage of the people.

Here the Christian element, indirectly apparent everywhere in Dickens's work, crystallizes round the Christmas

Excerpted from Louis Cazamian, "Dickens: Christmas Philosophy," translated by Stephen Wall from the 1904 original, *Le Roman Social in Angleterre*, and reprinted in *Charles Dickens: A Critical Anthology*, edited by Stephen Wall (Harmondsworth, U.K.: Penguin, 1970). Reprinted by permission of Stephen Wall.

festival. In the first story [*A Christmas Carol*] the birth of Christ itself becomes the symbol of a moral and social renewal. In *The Chimes* it is the church bells, the religious voices of the season, which preach to the poor their duties and their hopes; Christmas time merges with the turn of the year, the end of an unhappy past, the beginning of a better future. In both cases Dickens wanted to suggest a natural affinity between his gospel and this renewal of spirit and season. He felt and loved both the hushed contemplation and the overflowing joy of Christmas week deeply. No one has known better how to express the traditional feelings of a whole people. Strengthened by his sense of harmony with the national instinct, Dickens made a noble effort to expand it, and to employ it towards the peaceful solution of social problems. Christmas was already the supreme religious and family festival; on that day hearts opened, dead and withered feelings revived, souls were touched by pity, and separated, divided families came together round the parental hearth. Why not similarly unite, in heart and soul, the hostile brothers of the great national family? If this day has a magic which prompts goodness, why not let it shine beyond the confines of the house on everyone, the suffering, the defeated, the poor and the humble? If physical intoxication itself, groaning boards, roaring fires, trees hung with toys, the innocent happiness of children, and the fluttering of young girls kissed under the mistletoe, are healthy and good because they rekindle a joy in living, why not give a thought to those who on that day suffer more than ever from hunger and cold? In this way the Christian festival, a time of moral transformation, becomes the centre of a spreading and widening charity; the Christmas Stories make the connexion in Dickens between Christianity and social doctrine clearly discernible.

## PROPER ATTITUDES OF THE RICH AND THE POOR

On the constructive side this doctrine is extremely simple. Between men there exists a natural fellowship established by moral duties inseparable from religious feeling. This ought to reveal itself by the active concern which members of society show for each other; rich and poor have their duties. The latter already possess unsuspected virtues; among them devotion and self-sacrifice prosper; they are better, when they could so naturally be worse. But it is still necessary for them to make the most difficult effort of all: to maintain, along

with charity, faith and hope; to resist despair and social hatred. Dickens condemns, even if he understands, revolutionary violence. William Fern comes from Dorset, like the six
Tolpuddle martyrs; through him the author both accounts
for and disapproves of agrarian riots.[1] Nowhere is there any
question of Chartism.[2] Toby Veck[3] is severely punished for
having mistrusted human nature, and for being involuntar-
ily the sport of oppressors of the people and of agitators.
Courageous energy and steady hope ought to allow the poor
to look forward to the just rewards that the future holds for
them. Such rewards will not come of themselves; the rich,
the fortunate, and the powerful should do their utmost to
correct social injustices. How will they act? Dickens has no
thought of doing away with inequalities of wealth; he seems
to have had only a vague conception of the socialist ideal, as
if it was one of the fanciful dreams of revolution. But the appeal which the poor make to the rich has the strength of a legitimate demand. Dickens, like the leaders of the new philanthropy, acknowledged the right to relief. The governing
classes are responsible for social evils; over the ignorant and
the weak they have the natural authority of a father over his
children. It is necessary for the individual and the State to intervene in the life of the lower classes; private or public charity, devoted, sincere and patient action, must assuage and
cure without respite. The first Christmas Story especially in-
structs the rich in their duties. No deed is without value, no
goodwill useless. From the highest to the lowest, all those in
authority have the cure of souls. If Scrooge, the businessman,
increases the salary of Bob Cratchit, his clerk, he will have
made a contribution to social peace; if all employers were
like old Fezziwig, and treated their workers in a friendly
way, there would be less bitter hatred. Within the limits of
things as they are and the system as it is, society's physical
and spiritual scars must fade away. Otherwise, the abyss between the classes will deepen every day, and the already impending revolution will sweep away both rich and poor. And
Dickens had a clear picture of this social catastrophe taken
from Carlyle's epic *The French Revolution*. One of his novels
[*A Tale of Two Cities*] plainly reflects this influence.

1. In 1833–34, laborers agitated for higher wages, an action stopped by the government
when they prosecuted the Tolpuddle six.    2. Between 1837 and 1848 Chartists—
working-class reformers—tried to obtain the right to vote and be represented in Parliament.    3. a character in Dickens's *The Chimes*

The negative aspect of this doctrine is even clearer. It grapples with two enemies. One is 'stupid' Conservatism, the party of sheer habit, instinctively and selfishly reactionary. Here Dickens's radicalism is apparent in his revolt against a proud and overbearing philanthropy. He includes aristocratic socialism among the vain and hypocritical forms of charity. Sir Joseph Bowley obviously belongs to the Young England movement. But Dickens's main effort was not at all in this direction. He was displeased by the insulting manner of feudal benevolence, but at bottom he did not think it essential that the people should emancipate themselves: for him, as for Carlyle, salvation must come from above. One ought to remember his friendship with Lord Ashley; and it should be noted that the campaign of the 'Corn-Law League'[4]—preeminently a radical, middle-class movement—nowhere figures in his novels.

## THE REAL ENEMY: INDIVIDUALISM

The fact is that it was the work of radical individualists, and individualism was the enemy against which Dickens swore the most inveterate hostility. He invariably exposed it and fought against it in all its forms: economic dogmatism, utilitarian theory, middle-class custom. He loathed it on instinct, since it was the social manifestation of an inner coldness poles apart from his own emotional temperament; through feeling, since it was contrary to morality and Christian charity; through reason, in so far as he did reason, since it was the theory of selfishness. In the uncompromising and premature application of mathematics to life represented by the Malthusian Filer,[5] he sensed rather than understood an exaggerated and dangerous theory; and the practical 'common sense' of the alderman, the cold and pitiless vision of material interest, seemed to him a moral impoverishment of a similar kind and effect. His intuition made him sense the link between the emotional aridity of the businessman and the tyranny of narrow abstractions among economists. Unable to refute the latter, he attacked the former. Dickens's whole work is a huge attempt to destroy the psychological effects on the public of an apathy based on reason, and to substitute a willingness to intervene based on emotion.

---

4. a group seeking to restrict importation of corn to help local farmers   5. Thomas Malthus developed a theory showing that population increases faster than the food supply unless population is checked by moral restraint or by war, famine, or disease.

# A Christmas Carol Criticizes England's Economic System

Edgar Johnson

*Edgar Johnson argues that despite all the festivity, warmth, and good cheer Dickens creates in A Christmas Carol, at heart the story is a sharp criticism of England's economic system. A system that values everything only in terms of money and usefulness damages individuals, classes of people, and society as a whole. Johnson says that Dickens uses symbol and allegory to urge greater emphasis on humane practices. Edgar Johnson has published biographical criticism of British novelists and this article was the center of his critical chapter on A Christmas Carol in Charles Dickens: His Tragedy and Triumph. He is the author of a biography of Dickens and Sir Walter Scott: The Great Unknown.*

Everyone knows Dickens's *Christmas Carol* for its colorful painting of a rosy fireside good cheer and warmth of feeling, made all the more vivid by the contrasting chill wintry darkness in which its radiant scenes are framed. Most readers realize too how characteristic of all Dickens's sentiments about the Christmas season are the laughter and tenderness and jollity he poured into the *Carol*. What is not so widely understood is that it was also consistently and deliberately created as a critical blast against the very rationale of industrialism and its assumptions about the organizing principles of society. It is an attack upon both the economic behavior of the nineteenth-century businessman and the supporting theory of doctrinaire utilitarianism.[1] As such it is a good deal more significant than the mere outburst of warm-hearted sentimentality it is often taken to be.

1. the belief that the value of a thing or action is determined by its usefulness or utility

Excerpted from Edgar Johnson, "*The Christmas Carol* and the Economic Man," *American Scholar*, vol. 21 (1952). Reprinted by permission of the Estate of the late Edgar Johnson.

Its sharper intent is, indeed, ingeniously disguised. Not even the festivities at Dingley Dell, in *Pickwick Papers,* seem to have a more genial innocence than the scenes of the *Christmas Carol.* It is full of the tang of snow and cold air and crisp green holly-leaves, and warm with the glow of crimson holly-berries, blazing hearths, and human hearts. Deeper than this, however, Dickens makes of the Christmas spirit a symbolic criticism of the relations that throughout almost all the rest of the year subsist among men. It is a touchstone, revealing and drawing forth the gold of generosity ordinarily crusted over with selfish habit, an earnest of the truth that our natures are not entirely or even essentially devoted to competitive struggle.

Dickens is certain that the enjoyment most men are able to feel in the happiness of others can play a larger part than it does in the tenor of their lives. The sense of brotherhood, he feels, can be broadened to a deeper and more active concern for the welfare of all mankind. It is in this light that Dickens sees the Spirit of Christmas. So understood, as the distinguished scholar Professor Louis Cazamian rightly points out, his "philosophie de Noël" becomes the very core of his social thinking.

Not that Christmas has for Dickens more than the very smallest connection with Christian dogma or theology. It involves no conception of the virgin birth or transubstantiation[2] or sacrificial atonement or redemption by faith. For Dickens Christmas is primarily a human, not a supernatural, feast, with glowing emphasis on goose and gravy, plum-pudding and punch, mistletoe, and kissing-games, dancing and frolic, as well as open-handedness, sympathy, and warmth of heart. Dickens does not believe that love of others demands utter abnegation or mortification of the flesh; it is not sadness but joyful fellowship. The triumphal meaning of Christmas peals in the angel voices ringing through the sky: "On earth peace, good will to men." It is a sign that men do not live by bread alone, that they do not live for barter and sale alone. No way of life is either true or rewarding that leaves out men's need of loving and of being loved.

The theme of the *Christmas Carol* is thus closely linked with the theme of *Martin Chuzzlewit,* which was being written and published as a serial during the very time in which

2. the doctrine that the bread and wine of the Eucharist are transformed into the body and blood of Christ, though their appearance remains the same

the shorter story appeared. The selfishness so variously manifested in the one is limited in the other to the selfishness of financial gain. For in an acquisitive society the form that selfishness predominantly takes is monetary greed. The purpose of such a society is the protection of property rights. Its rules are created by those who have money and power, and are designed, to the extent that they are consistent, for the perpetuation of money and power. With the growing importance of commerce in the eighteenth century, and of industry in the nineteenth, political economists—the "philosophers" Dickens detested—rationalized the spirit of ruthless greed into a system claiming authority throughout society.

Services as well as goods, they said, were subject only to the laws of profitable trade. There was no just price. One bought in the cheapest market and sold in the dearest. There was no just wage. The mill owner paid the mill hand what competition decreed under the determination of the "iron law of wage." If the poor, the insufficiently aggressive, and the mediocre in ability were unable to live on what they could get, they must starve—or put up with the treadmill and the workhouse—and even these institutions represented concessions to mere humanity that must be made as forbidding as possible. Ideally, no sentimental conceptions must be allowed to obstruct the workings of the law of supply and demand. "Cash-nexus" was the sole bond between man and man. The supreme embodiment of this social theory was the notion of the "economic man," that curiously fragmentary picture of human nature, who never performed any action except at the dictates of monetary gain. And Scrooge, in the *Christmas Carol,* is nothing other than a personification of economic man.

Scrooge's entire life is limited to cash-boxes, ledgers, and bills of sale. He underpays and bullies and terrifies his clerk, and grudges him even enough coal in his office fire to keep warm. All sentiment, kindness, generosity, tenderness, he dismisses as humbug. All imagination he regards as a species of mental indigestion. He feels that he has discharged his full duty to society in contributing his share of the taxes that pay for the prison, the workhouse, the operation of the treadmill and the poor law, and he bitterly resents having his pocket picked to keep even them going. The out-of-work and the indigent sick are to him merely idle and useless; they had better die and decrease the surplus population. So entirely does Scrooge exemplify the economic man that, like that abstraction, his grasping rapacity has ceased to have any purpose beyond itself: when he closes up his office for the night he takes his pinched heart off to a solitary dinner at a tavern and then to his bleak chambers where he sits alone over his gruel.

## THE LIMITATIONS OF A SYSTEM BASED ON ECONOMIC GREED

Now from one angle, of course, *A Christmas Carol* indicts the economic philosophy represented by Scrooge for its unhappy influence on society. England's prosperity was not so uncertain—if, indeed, any nation's ever is—that she needed to be parsimonious and cruel to her waifs and strays, or even to the incompetents and casualties of life. To neglect the poor, to deny them education, to give them no protection from covetous employers, to let them be thrown out of work and fall ill and die in filthy surroundings that then engender spreading pestilence, to allow them to be harried by misery into crime—all these turn out in the long run to be the most disastrous shortsightedness.

That is what the Ghost of Christmas Present means in showing Scrooge the two ragged and wolfish children glaring from beneath its robes. "They are Man's," says the Spirit. "And they cling to me, appealing from their fathers. This boy is Ignorance. This girl is Want. Beware them both, and all of their degree, but most of all beware this boy, for on his brow I see that written which is Doom, unless the writing be erased." And when Scrooge asks if they have no refuge, the Spirit ironically echoes his own words: "Are there no prisons? Are there no workhouses?"

Scrooge's relation with his clerk Bob Cratchit is another illustration of the same point. To say, as some commentators have done, that Scrooge is paying Cratchit all he is worth on the open market (or he would get another job) is to assume the very conditions Dickens is attacking. It is not only that timid, uncompetitive people like Bob Cratchit may lack the courage to bargain for their rights. But, as Dickens knows well, there are many things other than the usefulness of a man's work that determine his wage—the existence, for example, of a large body of other men able to do the same job. And if Cratchit is getting the established remuneration for his work, that makes the situation worse, not better; for instead of an isolated one, his is a general case. What Dickens has at heart is not any economic conception like Marx's labor theory of value, but a feeling of the human value of human beings. Unless a man is a noxious danger to society, Dickens feels, a beast of prey to be segregated or destroyed, if he is able and willing to work, whatever the work may be—he is entitled at least to enough for him to live on, by the mere virtue of his humanity alone.

But the actual organization that Dickens saw in society callously disregarded all such humane principles. The hardened criminal was maintained in jail with more care than the helpless debtor who had broken no law. The pauper who owed nobody, but whom age, illness, or industrial change might have thrown out of work, was treated more severely than many a debtor and jailbird. And the poor clerk or laborer, rendered powerless by his need or the number of others like him, could be held to a pittance barely sufficient to keep him and his family from starvation.

Against such inequities Dickens maintains that any work worth doing should be paid enough to maintain a man and his family without grinding worry. How are the Bob Cratchits and their helpless children to live? Or are we to let the crippled Tiny Tims die and decrease the surplus population? "Man," says the Ghost, "if man you be in heart, not adamant, forbear that wicked cant until you have discovered What the surplus is and Where it is. . . . It may be, that in the sight of Heaven, you are more worthless and less fit to live than millions like this poor man's child. Oh God! to hear the Insect on the leaf pronouncing on the too much life among his hungry brothers in the dust!"

Coldhearted arrogance and injustice storing up a dangerous heritage of poverty and ignorance—such is Dickens's judgment of the economic system that Scrooge exemplifies. But its consequences do not end with the cruelties it inflicts upon the masses of the people or the evils it works in society. It injures Scrooge as well. All the more generous impulses of humanity he has stifled and mutilated in himself. All natural affection he has crushed. The lonely boy he used to be, weeping in school, the tender brother, the eager youth, the young man who once fell disinterestedly in love with a dowerless girl—what has he done to them in making himself into a money-making machine, as hard and sharp as flint, and frozen with the internal ice that clutches his shriveled heart? That dismal cell, his office, and his gloomy rooms, are only a prison within which he dwells self-confined, barred and close-locked as he drags a chain of his own cash-boxes and dusty ledgers. Acting on a distortedly inadequate conception of self-interest, Scrooge has deformed and crippled himself to bitter sterility.

---

### SCROOGE COLDER THAN BAD WEATHER

*Dickens's descriptive language makes Scrooge a symbol of prevailing economic values and all that is cold and indifferent toward human beings.*

Oh! But he was a tight-fisted hand at the grindstone, Scrooge! a squeezing, wrenching, grasping, scraping, clutching, covetous, old sinner! Hard and sharp as flint, from which no steel had ever struck out generous fire; secret, and self-contained, and solitary as an oyster. The cold within him froze his old features, nipped his pointed nose, shrivelled his cheek, stiffened his gait; made his eyes red, his thin lips blue; and spoke out shrewdly in his grating voice. A frosty rime was on his head, and on his eyebrows, and his wiry chin. He carried his own low temperature always about with him; he iced his office in the dog-days; and didn't thaw it one degree at Christmas.

External heat and cold had little influence on Scrooge. No warmth could warm, nor wintry weather chill him. No wind that blew was bitterer than he, no falling snow was more intent upon its purpose, no pelting rain less open to entreaty. Foul weather didn't know where to have him. The heaviest rain, and snow, and hail, and sleet, could boast of the advantage over him in only one respect. They often 'came down' handsomely, and Scrooge never did.

Nobody ever stopped him in the street to say, with gladsome looks, "My dear Scrooge, how are you? . . ."

---

And Scrooge's fallacy is the fallacy of organized society. Like his house, which Dickens fancifully imagines playing hide-and-seek with other houses when it was a young house, and losing its way in a blind alley it has forgotten how to get out of, Scrooge has lost his way between youth and maturity. Society too in the course of its development has gone astray and then hardened itself in obdurate error with a heartless economic theory. Scrooge's conversion is more than the transformation of a single human being. It is a plea for society itself to undergo a change of heart.

Dickens does not, it should be noticed, take the uncompromising position that the self-regarding emotions are to be eradicated altogether. He is not one of those austere theorists who hold that the individual must be subordinated to the state or immolate himself to the service of an abstract humanity. Concern for one's self and one's own welfare is necessary and right, but true self-love cannot be severed from love of others without growing barren and diseased. Only in the communion of brotherhood is it healthy and fruitful. When Scrooge has truly changed, and has dispatched the anonymous gift of the turkey to Bob Cratchit as an earnest of repentance, his next move is to go to his nephew's house and ask wistfully, "Will you let me in, Fred?" With love reanimated in his heart, he may hope for love.

There have been readers who objected to Scrooge's conversion as too sudden and radical to be psychologically convincing. But this is to mistake a semi-serious fantasy for a piece of prosaic realism. Even so, the emotions in Scrooge to which the Ghosts appeal are no unsound means to the intended end: the awakened memories of a past when he had known warmer and gentler ties than in any of his later years, the realization of his exclusion from all kindness and affection in others now, the fears of a future when he may be lonelier and more unloved still. And William James in *The Varieties of Religious Experience* provides scores of case-histories that parallel both the suddenness of Scrooge's conversion and the sense of radiant joy he feels in the world around him after it has taken place. It may be that what really gives the skeptics pause is that Scrooge is converted to a gospel of good cheer. They could probably believe easily enough if he espoused some gloomy doctrine of intolerance.

But it is doubtful whether such questions ever arise when one is actually reading the *Christmas Carol*. From the very beginning Dickens strikes a tone of playful exaggeration that warns us this is no exercise in naturalism. Scrooge carries "his own low temperature always about with him; he iced his office in the dog-days." Blind men's dogs, when they see him coming, tug their masters into doorways to avoid him. The entire world of the story is an animistic one: houses play hide-and-seek, door-knockers come to life as human heads, the tuning of a fiddle is "like fifty stomach aches," old Fezziwig's legs wink as he dances, potatoes bubbling in a saucepan knock loudly at the lid "to be let out and peeled." Scrooge's own language has a jocose hyperbole, even when he is supposed to be most ferocious or most terrified, that makes his very utterance seem half a masquerade. "If I could work my will," he snarls, "every idiot who goes about with 'Merry Christmas' on his lips should be boiled with his own pudding, and buried with a stake of holly through his heart. He should!" Is that the accent of a genuine curmudgeon or of a man trying to sound more violent than he feels? And to Marley's Ghost, despite his disquiet, he remarks, "You may be an undigested bit of beef, a blob of mustard, a crumb of cheese, a fragment of an underdone potato. There's more of gravy than of grave about you, whatever you are!"

## THE STORY AS AN ALLEGORY

All these things make it clear that Dickens—as always when he is most deeply moved and most profound—is speaking in terms of unavowed allegory.... Dickens, however, leaves his surface action so entirely clear and the behavior of his characters so plain that they do not puzzle us into groping for gnomic meanings. Scrooge is a miser, his nephew a warmhearted fellow, Bob Cratchit a poor clerk—what could be simpler? If there is a touch of oddity in the details, that is merely Dickens's well-known comic grotesquerie; if Scrooge's change of heart is sharp and antithetical, that is only Dickens's melodramatic sentimentality. Surely all the world knows that Dickens is never profound?

But the truth is that Dickens has so fused his abstract thought and its imaginative forming that one melts almost entirely into the other. Though our emotional perception of Dickens's meaning is immediate and spontaneous, nothing in his handling thrusts upon us an intellectual statement of that meaning. But more than a warmhearted outpouring of holiday sentiment, the *Christmas Carol* is in essence a serio-comic parable of social redemption. Marley's Ghost is the symbol of divine grace, and the three Christmas Spirits are the working of that grace through the agencies of memory, example and fear. And Scrooge, although of course he is himself too, is not himself alone: he is the embodiment of all that concentration upon material power and callous indifference to the welfare of human beings that the economists had erected into a system, businessmen and industrialists pursued relentlessly, and society taken for granted as inevitable and proper. The conversion of Scrooge is an image of the conversion for which Dickens hopes among mankind.

# CHAPTER 3

# Dickens's Semiauto-biographical Novels

READINGS ON
CHARLES DICKENS

# Poverty in *Oliver Twist*

Humphry House

Humphry House's analysis relates the themes and characters in *Oliver Twist* to the personal background of Charles Dickens and to the social conditions of the poor in England during the 1830s. House maintains that Oliver is as lonely and abused as Dickens was as a child and that the workhouse conditions in Oliver's background depict the real conditions of England's underclass when the novel was published in serial form. Humphry House worked on an edition of Dickens's letters, but he died suddenly before completing the task. He is best known for *The Dickens World*, published in 1941.

Dickens began *Oliver Twist* as a serial in *Bentley's Miscellany,* of which he had just become editor, in February 1837. He was a young man of twenty-five, full of confidence and energy, who had suddenly found himself famous and was very pleased about it. . . .

The declared subject was intensely topical and, by chance, the course of events made it more so as the publication proceeded. The controversies, alarms, hardships, and bitternesses which attended the introduction of the new Poor Law in 1834 may now seem remote; but *Oliver Twist* cannot be fully understood without remembering that it was planned and begun in an atmosphere of heightened public interest and of anxiety which deepened as the story ran.

It was Dickens's first attempt at a novel proper. The sequence of the external events which befall Oliver and form the framework of the book, though improbable, is at least straightforward, organized, and fairly well proportioned; but all the subordinate matter designed to explain and account for these events is at once complicated and careless. . . .

The unity of the book derives from impulse and from the energy of its imagination, not from its construction.

Reprinted from The Oxford Illustrated Dickens edition (1949) of *The Adventures of Oliver Twist* by permission of Oxford University Press.

Superficially the impulse would appear mainly didactic and moral; and it was this aspect of the story that Dickens himself emphasized in the Preface which he first wrote for the edition of 1841. In that Preface he concentrated on his portraiture of thieves and murderers and prostitutes 'as they really were, for ever skulking uneasily through the dirtiest paths of life, with the great black ghastly gallows closing up their prospect'. He suggested that such realism in itself would perform a 'service to society'. He was then answering critics, like Richard Ford in *The Quarterly Review,* who said 'we object *in toto* to the staple of *Oliver Twist*—a series of representations which must familiarize the rising generation with the haunts, deeds, language and characters of the very dregs of the community. . . . It is a hazardous experiment to exhibit to the young these enormities, even on the Helot principle[1] of inspiring disgust.'

Dickens's answer was, in effect, a plea for broadening the whole scope of prose fiction, for the abandonment of false attitudes. Low life and criminal life exist, he argues, and nothing but a healthier frame of mind can follow from the knowledge of them. The technique and tone of what came to be called realism vary from generation to generation; speech tabus are inconstant; even the forms in which moral purpose is expressed are largely a matter of fashion. Allowing for such changes in custom, we must recognize in *Oliver,* besides its own inherent qualities, a novel which permanently affected the range, status, and potentialities of fiction. Even Ford admitted as much when he wrote:

> Life in London, as revealed in the pages of Boz, opens a new world to thousands bred and born in the same city, whose palaces overshadow their cellars—for the one half of mankind lives without knowing how the other half dies: in fact, the regions about Saffron Hill are less known to our great world than the Oxford Tracts; the inhabitants are still less. . . .

The 'revelations' in the novel were not in themselves by any means new: Dickens was not in that way a pioneer: he used material that was fairly well known, and ready to hand. The Saffron Hill district was notorious, among those who were inquisitive or needed to know, as the haunt of pickpockets and thieves. . . . The appalling filth of the slums in that area had been familiar in the cholera epidemic of 1832. . . .

---

1. a system of keeping a class of nominally free people oppressed

It was also common knowledge that young recruits for gangs of thieves were most commonly enticed by girls of the Nancy type, who haunted lodging-houses and pubs like 'The Three Cripples'. In his knowledge of such things Dickens was by no means unique; but using it in a novel, with all the heightened interest of a vivid story, he brought it home to the drawing-rooms and studies and boudoirs where ignorance, blissful and delicate, might be touched. In *The Newcomes*, Thackeray[2] made Lady Walham take *Oliver Twist* secretively to her bedroom.

## THE EMOTIONAL APPEAL OF OLIVER AND NANCY

Some vague stirring in the intelligence or conscience was indeed all that the novel could be expected to achieve; for a serious, considered moral lesson is very hard to find. If the purpose were to show that the starvation and cruel ill-treatment of children in baby-farms and workhouses produced ghastly effects on their characters and in society, then Oliver should have turned out a monster or a wretch, a boy who did very well at Fagin's school. Instead of this he remained always a paragon of sweet gratitude and the tenderest right feeling: at school he was distinguished for invincible greenness and showed no skill or even promise in bringing back fogles and tickers.[3] When it has finally been disclosed that Oliver's parents were an unhappy gentleman of means and the daughter of a naval officer, are we to conclude that Dickens's main lesson was that a good heredity can overcome anything, and that in some cases environment counts for nothing at all? He probably never even asked himself the question in that form; from his other work—more perhaps from his journalism and speeches than from his novels—we know that all his emphasis was on the physical environment generally; but Oliver and Nancy teach the opposite; it was a dilemma he never fully faced and certainly never solved.

But Dickens's most revealing comment on *Oliver* was not in his Preface. For four years in the prime of his life he practically abandoned writing, gave rein to his exhibitionism, his histrionic and mesmeric powers, and poured his prodigious energies into public readings from his own works. The effect

2. British writer William   3. pocket-handkerchiefs, watches, and trinkets—valuables acquired by pick pocketing

was that of a complete, competent, highly emotional theatrical performance. As time went on he developed an increasing desire to read 'The Murder of Nancy' from *Oliver Twist.* 'I have no doubt', he wrote, 'that I could perfectly petrify an audience by carrying out the notion I have of the way of rendering it.' He had known for thirty years that the whole episode was charged with emotional dynamite.... The theme of murder, and still more of the murderer being hunted and haunted after his crime, treated not as a detective story, but as a statement of human behaviour, recurs several times in his major work. Both Sikes and Jonas Chuzzlewit are transfigured by the act of murder.

## THE PSYCHOLOGY OF THE OUTCAST

The psychological condition of a rebel-reformer is in many ways similar to that of a criminal, and may have the same origins. A feeling of being outside the ordinary organization of group life; a feeling of being an outcast, a misfit or a victim of circumstance; a feeling of bitter loneliness, isolation, ostracism or irrevocable disgrace—any one or any combination of such feelings may turn a man against organized society, and his opposition may express itself in what is technically crime or what is technically politics: treason, sedition, and armed rebellion manage to be both. Dickens's childhood had been such that all these feelings, at different times in different degrees, had been his: he knew no security and no tenderness: the family home was for a time the Marshalsea prison, and for six months Dickens himself was a wretched drudge in a blacking-factory. These two experiences, and others similar, lie behind the loneliness, disgrace and outlawry which pervade all his novels. These were always his leading psychological themes. *Oliver Twist* reveals them in an early stage, not fully developed, certainly not analysed, but very clear. Oliver himself is so much the mere embodiment of the idea of a lonely ill-used child that he is scarcely granted character enough to be anything else....

It is not merely true that Fagin, Sikes, Nancy, and even the Dodger are treated with more intelligence and interest in the novel than any other characters; they are also treated, in the deepest sense, with more sympathy. Dickens is prepared to take infinite pains to follow the working of their minds, to clarify their policies and motives, to give their personalities scope in the descriptions of all that they do or suffer. The absence of this sort of sympathy in the treatment of Monks, whose melodramatic and inefficient malignity is contemptuously devised to supply the mechanism of the tale, brings out the point by contrast. Fagin and Sikes are never despised, even though what they do is despicable. The cringing meanness of the one and the unmitigated coarse brutality of the other are treated with immense and serious respect: Dickens lives into these characters as they grow. At the crisis in the life of each there is no question of moralizing or preaching: Dickens identifies himself with them; he himself is the lonely outcast capable of crime. Fagin in the dock, when 'the court was paved, from floor to roof, with human faces', when 'in no one face—not even among the women, of whom there were many there—could he read the faintest sympathy with himself', is a figure of the most terrifying loneliness; and the jumping of his mind from detail to detail—one man's clothes, another man's dinner, the broken spike—is the psychological counterpart of Sikes's haunted wandering in the country north of London. In Sikes the criminal impulse is cruder and more violent: but Dickens's understanding is not less. The atmosphere of horror is achieved just because of his fear that he might do exactly such a murder as Sikes did. During the famous readings he used to speak jokingly of giving way to his 'murderous instincts'; but it was no joke.

The lasting impression left by this novel is one of macabre horror. For us there appears to be little connexion between the mood and incidents of the later chapters, and those of the earlier. We begin to wonder whether perhaps, as the Fagin-Sikes themes took hold upon him, Dickens was liable to forget his sub-title, 'The Parish Boy's Progress'. But to an alert reader in 1837–9 the factual and emotional connexion between the beginning and the end would have seemed far stronger: the mood of the book was topical.

## ENGLISH SOCIETY AND THE POOR LAW OF 1834

The 'philosophers', with blood of ice and hearts of iron, on whom Dickens pours his sarcasm in the early chapters, were the Malthusians and economists, whose theory of population underlay the new Poor Law of 1834. Their doctrine briefly was that, however much the general wealth of the country grew, there would always be a section of the population below subsistence level, because of an inevitable natural tendency of population to increase faster than the means of subsistence. Vice and misery were the two first checks on the multiplication of unwanted mouths; the only third possible check was moral or prudential restraint, which meant the prevention, by one means or another, of breeding in the poorest classes. All forms of dole, charity or relief to a man unable to maintain himself or his family were suspect, because they were a direct inducement to breed in idleness, and thus aided the dismal course of nature. If the preaching of thrift and continence failed, the only acceptable policy was to give relief in the most unattractive form, under conditions which made breeding impossible.

By the Act of 1834 the Parish remained the primary unit of administration, and relief depended on a parish 'settlement'. For Poor Law purposes parishes were formed into 'Unions'; each Union had its Workhouse, and a Board of Guardians to administer relief. But, as far as possible, relief was only to be given in the 'house'. Conditions there were deliberately made hard: the diet was sparse; husbands were separated from wives; a special uniform was worn, and so on. The 'Workhouse-test' was intended as a deterrent. Dickens does not discuss the rightness or wrongness of the basic theory, nor the evils of subsidizing wages from the rates which its application was largely designed to cure. He directs his angry sarcasm only to some of the human consequences of what was done.

The original Poor Law Commissioners, on whose findings the Act was drafted, had quite rightly urged that different classes of pauper needed different treatment. The old, the infirm, the insane, the diseased, unable to earn their own living, were a charge upon the community of a different kind from the able-bodied unemployed or the 'sturdy beggar'. Children in particular, and orphan children most of all, were plainly in a separate category, and no 'workhouse-test' could be held to apply to them. But, through inefficiencies and difficulties in the practical application of the Act, these proper distinctions did not generally lead to differences of treatment. The workhouse tended to remain the 'general-mixed' institution which had been such a scandal in the earlier days; people of both sexes, of all ages, all physical and moral conditions, were herded indiscriminately together, and treated like recalcitrant idlers, all equally kept on low diet: the deterrent system, meant only for the able-bodied, in practice put the screw on all alike. The children obviously suffered worst.

Oliver was born in a workhouse of the old law; when he came back from Mrs. Mann's, the new law had just come in and 'the Board' had just been set up. Dickens seems to have imagined the actual workhouse building unaltered, for the new 'Bastilles' were not built in a hurry; Bumble was probably meant to be a 'porochial officer' taken over from the old system: in these respects Dickens was attacking abuses allowed to continue. But the low diet was the one outstanding typical feature of the new system. Dickens's 'three meals of thin gruel a day, with an onion twice a week, and half a roll on Sundays' was a telling caricature of the Commissioners' recommended dietaries. To a modern reader, after the rationing of two wars, these dietaries do not, on paper, seem very terrible: but it is hard to say how they worked out in practice. Certainly they were very ill-balanced and dull. In the No. 1 Dietary for an able-bodied man, published in 1836, there was meat on only three days of a week, and 1½ pints of gruel every day. Women were to have less and children over nine the same as women; children under nine were to be dieted 'at discretion'. Contemporary opinion can be judged by the fact that in March 1838 the Guardians of the Dudley Union presented a petition to the House of Lords complaining that the diets recommended by the Commissioners were not enough to feed the paupers: and then already half the country was laughing or weeping over Oliver, who 'asked for more'. It also happened that in the third year of the new law there was a very severe winter; in the fourth a trade depression; and that the fifth was a year of scarce food and high prices. With these causes of hardship the unpopularity of the law grew, and *Oliver Twist* appeared to be not merely topical but prophetic.

Through administrative muddles and false economy, through conflicts between the central and local authorities, through jealousy of the central power, and most of all through the impotent fears engendered by Malthusian orthodoxy, the condition of pauper children remained appalling for many years after *Oliver Twist* was written. Dickens did not forget the image of the Good Samaritan on Bumble's buttons. As a journalist and editor he published many articles on the subject, the gist of which was summed up in *Household Words* in 1850:

> Ought the misdeeds of the parents to be visited on their innocent children? Should pauper and outcast infants be ne-

glected so as to become pests to Society . . . ? Common sense asks, does the State desire good citizens or bad?

*Oliver Twist* had been written in a period when the possibility of armed revolution was constantly before men's minds—there was in fact an abortive rising in 1839; and in that atmosphere the problems of the Poor Law had an urgency and horror which they lost in the relative security and peace of the mid-Victorian age. When Dickens came back to the book and gave the readings of the 'Murder', he had thirty years of burning life and imagination behind him: the obsessive interest in violent crime, registered on his pulse, was linked in memory both to the early Chartists[4] and the lynchings by Rebecca and her Daughters and also to the terrors and rebelliousness of a lonely outcast child, of whom the wretched Oliver himself was but a very pale and ineffectual reflection.

4. political reformers active in England between 1838 and 1848

# The Pattern of Good and Evil in *Oliver Twist*

Geoffrey Thurley

Acknowledging that *Oliver Twist* progresses in a series of coincidental events, Geoffrey Thurley finds a pattern in which good evolves from evil and vice versa. Thurley maintains that the novel's dreamlike logic mirrors the nightmare fear of poverty and evil, represented by Fagin, Sikes, and Monks, and the triumph of good, represented by the rescue and safety of Oliver. Geoffrey Thurley has taught at universities in Ireland, Poland, Australia, and England. He has written poetry and published *Quiet Flowers: Poems* and *White Flock: Poems.* He is also the author of *The Psychology of Hardy's Novels: The Nervous and the Statuesque* and *The American Moment: American Poetry in the Mid-Century.*

[In *Oliver Twist*] Dickens takes his hero from the workhouse to unending security by means of outrageous coincidence and smiling chance. If this implies a limiting criticism of the novel it also indicates the nature of its virtues. . . . What we have here is not a realistic novel creaking at the joints with absurd coincidences and long-lost relationships, but a novel governed from within by a different logic. . . . It is to its moral vision that we must attribute the enduring grip of a novel. . . .

Briefly summarized, the skeleton of the plot is as follows: Oliver, born in the workhouse, leaves his master (the undertaker Sowerberry) to "seek his fortune" in London; he falls in with the Artful Dodger, who takes him to Fagin's den; he is arrested for pickpocketing, then instated not in prison but in the middle-class paradise of his unknowing godfather; he is snatched back for Fagin by the prostitute Nancy; once more restored to safety and family through the failure of a housebreaking job he is forced to take part in by Bill Sikes;

Excerpted from *The Dickens Myth* by Geoffrey Thurley. Copyright ©1976 by Geoffrey John Thurley. Reprinted with permission of St. Martin's Press, Inc. (Notes in the original have been omitted here.)

is threatened one last time by Fagin and his own half-brother, Monks, but remains secure, while Fagin, Monks, and Sikes are all destroyed. That is more or less all. So presented it seems identical with innumerable cautionary tales penned by mid-Victorian do-gooders: at first sight, at least. When we take a closer look, even the skeleton reveals certain more interesting features.

## A PATTERN OF GOOD COMING OUT OF EVIL AND VICE VERSA

First, Oliver is rescued or captured in every case while he is engaged on someone else's project: the pickpocketing expedition with the Dodger and Charley Bates, the errand to the bookseller's for Mr. Brownlow, the Chertsey job for Sikes and Fagin. Every time Oliver changes worlds, in other words, it is through a misfiring of a plan. Moreover, the plans which misfire have consequences morally opposite to those intended. . . .

The evil is consistently a means of arriving at the good, and vice versa. The pattern runs right through the book. The sweep Gamfield's brutality is in part at least the cause of Oliver's falling under the kinder influence of Mr. Sowerberry; whose own kindness towards Oliver is again at least in part a cause of Noah Claypole's and Mrs. Sowerberry's hostility. When Oliver first arrives in London, the Artful Dodger—who picks him up in Barnet—shares his food with him; later, when Oliver is introduced into Fagin's den, the "Merry Old Gentleman" makes him laugh, feeds him, and gives him a roof and a bed. The purpose of all this hospitality is, ultimately, to corrupt him, but the immediate impression is of a spontaneous camaraderie which contrasts ironically with the coldness and inhumanity Oliver has known earlier in life. . . .

It is indeed just because Dickens so obviously wanted to write a happily-ever-after fairy-story with a few social pungencies on the side that the actual nightmarish plunges into the abyss and dreamlike emergences into light and cleanliness have such a powerful grip on the imagination. In writing *Oliver Twist* Dickens was possessed of deeper fears than he was consciously acquainted with: Oliver's swings into and out of the clutches of Fagin reveal, surely, a fascination with evil, sordidity, and degradation that exerts a frightening drawing-power on the mind. Like Dostoievsky,[1] Dickens invests evil

1. Russian novelist Fyodor

with a profound ambivalence, and this ambivalence is what is reflected in the rhythmic pattern of the narrative. . . .

## THE DREAMLIKE LOGIC IN THE NOVEL

It is commonplace nowadays to refer to *Oliver Twist* in terms of its dreamlike logic. . . . As sensible critic, G.K. Chesterton felt obliged to observe that the plot is "preposterous"; but there is no doubt that he felt the power of the novel's "dream" logic. We cannot, in point of fact, cut the book up into acceptable and preposterous elements (based upon some criterion of realistic verisimilitude) without destroying it altogether. For the power of the fable is expressed specifically in terms of dreamlike eventualities. . . .

When, some weeks after the return to Fagin's den, Oliver is taken out on the burgling expedition at Chertsey, the sequence we have just remarked upon—from light to darkness—is once again reversed: after the heightened nightmarishness of the robbery and the wounding—the blinding pain, the bewildering faces staring down at Oliver, Sikes from one side, the servants from the other—comes the dreamlike awakening again, accompanied by the well-remembered pleasant exhaustion: "The boy stirred and smiled in his sleep . . ." And this idyll is in its turn smashed by the sudden apparition of Fagin and Monks at Oliver's window. Considered in terms of probability, this casement scene is absurd: in its own dream terms, it is frighteningly effective. Fagin is in his true diabolical element suddenly appearing at a window. . . . The terror aroused by these scenes is of the very essence of the book's inner logic: the "unlikeliness" of these incidents does not threaten the tension, it creates it.

## THE UNDERLYING FEAR OF POVERTY AND EVIL

The source of the nightmare is, on one level, the dread of poverty and degradation underlying the myth of which this novel is, I have argued, the most naked enactment in all Dickens. But this polarity of darkness and light, poverty and affluence, violence and tranquillity, possesses a spiritual counterpart. In articulating so brilliantly the Victorian fear of poverty and lost-ness, Dickens at the same time enunciated a religious parable of great beauty and purity: it is the human soul which is threatened in the person of Oliver Twist, that soul which modern man has so much feared to lose in his new urban, technological, and commercial environment. *Oliver Twist* is about the soul of man under capitalism, but it is also about the soul of man under the constant and perennial pressure of evil. It is not so much that we can see the sequence of events making up the narrative "in two ways", or on two planes, as that we cannot fully understand them unless both the social and the spiritual aspects are taken into account together. Now Dickens is remarkably free with words and images which dictate a quasi-religious interpretation. In no other Dickens novel is evil more powerfully evil, or good more radiantly and unequivocally good. The action makes up, in fact, an astonishingly natural and unadorned morality.

The devil is of course more "interesting", and Fagin is without question one of the most powerful and pregnant embodiments of evil in nineteenth-century fiction. In Fagin we are brought into direct contact with evil. The apprehension is instinctive and simple, but what is apprehended is compound, a rich amalgam of attraction and revulsion. Fagin possessed an innate charisma, a charm, almost, which fascinates Oliver. It is curious in fact that at no point does Dickens say that Fagin repels Oliver or show Oliver recoiling from him. . . .

[The] narrative . . . really has only one subject: the safety of Oliver Twist. It is a remarkable achievement to sustain so intense an interest upon such a fragile basis. . . . Yet this sparseness of narrative material, far from being a weakness, is precisely the secret of its excellence. The narrative flickers with apprehension whenever Oliver's security is threatened; a large number of the secondary characters in the novel exist only to menace Oliver—Noah Claypole, Mrs. Sowerberry, Bumble himself, Mr. Fang the magistrate, Gamfield. In no other Dickens novel are there so many overheard conversations or eavesdroppings; people are tailed and watched—and if they are not actually, they imagine they are.

## THE FUNCTION OF MONKS

This is all spectacularly true of Fagin's aide, Monks, Oliver's half-brother, whose machinations against him provide the novel's major action. Monks is in fact a minor study of a major nineteenth-century preoccupation—the satanic personality. . . . He is, we learn, "tall and dark"; his eye is "keen and bright, but shadowed by a scowl of distrust and suspicion, . . . and repulsive to behold" (Chapter 37). During a conversation with Bumble, Monks refers to himself as a friend of the devil. . . .

For this Dostoievskian epileptic has his own hallucinatory obsessions, which counterbalance the fears and terrors of Oliver himself. Oliver in fact causes Monks an irrational horror which transcends the financial threat he represents. Oliver pops up to wreck Monks's peace of mind (such as it could be) as inevitably as Fagin shatters Oliver's. . . . After more provoking innocence from Oliver, Monks falls to the ground in the throes of a fit. The reaction seems disproportionate to the facts: in part, indeed, it is, and Dickens displays considerable skill in holding the neurotic obsessions before us for long periods before finally divulging their factual basis. When, at the end of the book, the story behind Oliver's parentage is finally revealed, partly by Mr. Brownlow and partly by Monks himself in an enforced confession, this impression is intensified: Monks was the legitimate son of Edwin Leeford, Oliver the illegitimate son of Leeford and Agnes Fleming (the book should by rights be called Oliver Leeford, but Mr. Bumble's invention holds its place even after the revelations of chapter 51). By a late will, Leeford had left all his money to Oliver and his mother. Monks's mother burned this will, but she was obsessed with the idea that a son had been born: Monks had sworn to "hunt it down; never to let it rest; to pursue it with the bitterest and most unrelenting animosity; to vent upon it the hatred that I deeply felt and to spit upon the empty vaunt of that insulting will by dragging it, if I could, to the very gallows-foot" (Chapter 51). It is hardly possible to reconcile the nebulous threat Oliver might possibly have posed (could the will have been remembered or revived) with the morbid ferocity of Monks's hatred: once again, it seems impossible to understand the novel without a religious or theological interpretation. We note that the will is "insulting" to Monks: he takes up his dead mother's cause with a puritanic zeal, a zeal engendered half by wounded pride, half by an innate hostility towards what is felt to be a more pure relationship. Monks cannot tolerate the very existence of the "natural" child: he wants to rid the world of its goodness. . . .

Monks puts on a tremendous display of satanic malice; he remains totally unrepentant, and his contempt for Mr. Brownlow, like his hatred of Oliver, emerges even more strongly from these explanations as being of an absolute and

indissoluble kind. Like Ahab's obsession with the White
Whale, Monks's fixation on destroying Oliver transcends all
rational motivation: he loathes his half-brother as evil
loathes good.

It is unquestionably the theological dimension in which
Monks has his being that saves the character from unreality,
even in scenes when Dickens overplays his hand. This is
true for instance of chapter 38 where Monks keeps his ren-
dezvous with the Bumbles: it is a "dark and stormy night",
the surroundings are evilly sordid, beneath their feet flows a
"turbid" stream. Monks is in his element, and all but
gnashes his teeth—"'Hear it!' he cries, when the thunder
rolls, 'hear it! Rolling and crashing on as if it echoed through
a thousand caverns where the devils were hiding from it. I
hate the sound!'"...

A peculiarly disturbing feature of Monks's satanism is
that he does not want Oliver killed, but corrupted. True, he
gives as his reason for not wanting the boy murdered that
the blood will haunt him, and this dread suits his morbid
temperament. But it is not difficult to understand why having Oliver murdered (easily done, and far more rational
from the point of view of Monks's threatened inheritance)
would not satisfy him: it would confirm Oliver in his innocence, and what Monks needs is to defile this innocence,
and prove Oliver no better than himself. Monks expresses
this desire to have Oliver corrupted most vehemently in the
conversation with Fagin in chapter 26....

Monks's desire to have Oliver corrupted—overheard by
Nancy in the event—counterpoints Nancy's own growing
remorse at having been instrumental in bringing Oliver
back to Fagin's den and the life of crime. Nancy had already
intervened on Oliver's behalf immediately on restoring him
to Fagin: it is now that the old Jew starts beating Oliver and
the action precipitates her own inward change. When
Nancy springs to his defence, the process of regret that is to
end in her death commences. It is, as I have said, her having been instrumental in bringing Oliver to the threshold of
corruption that first awakens her own sense of what she
herself has become.... It is herself she sees in Oliver, and
upon being reminded by Fagin that the thieving and prostitution he introduced her to has been a living, she retorts: "It
is my living; and the cold, wet, dirty streets are my home;
and you're the wretch that drove me to them long ago, and

that'll keep me there, day and night, day and night till I die!" (Chapter 16) . . .

## NANCY AND ROSE MAYLIE AS FOILS FOR OLIVER AND NOAH CLAYPOLE

Oliver's innocence and purity not only arouse her pity, but force her into an awareness of what she herself is. This awareness is still more poignantly aroused by the sight of Rose Maylie in the west end hotel. Nancy has been bitterly insulted by the servants of the hotel, and when she hears Rose's footsteps at last, she falls into a panic of shame. . . . The whole scene is beautifully managed, a superb confrontation of the soiled and the pure, in which each party watches its own anti-self in the other. . . . Without Nancy, Rose Maylie is a china doll; without Rose, Nancy an incomplete "fallen woman". Bringing the two images together Dickens poignantly evokes a full image of moral decline, through no personal weakness, but through the action of a "wasting life". . . .

The scene in the west end hotel leads directly to Nancy's death. Her end is in the event brought about through the agency of Noah Claypole. Claypole's reappearance late in the novel seems a mistake, until we realize that he makes a strange parody of the basic Dick Whittington role that Oliver has already played. Like Oliver, Noah arrives in London by the Great North Road; he is first observed pausing beneath the archway at Highgate, which is traditionally associated, as Dickens later ironically observes *à propos* of Sikes, with Dick Whittington. Noah's intention is the same as Oliver's—to seek his fortune in London; and he fits the part of the country bumpkin—with his "long-limbed, knock kneed, shambling, bony" look, the dust on his boots, the guileless arrogance and the vaguely Midland accent—much better than Oliver. This is no doubt his function: to provide the kind of focussing opposite for Oliver which Nancy, in different ways, had provided for Rose Maylie. But for circumstances, Nancy might have been Rose Maylie; but for character, Oliver might have been Noah Claypole. . . .

## THE POWERS OF EVIL DESTROYED

With the eavesdropping scene on London Bridge, the powers of evil start working out their own destruction. Noah Claypole's report to Fagin leads directly to the murder of Nancy,

the flight and death of Sikes, and Fagin's own arrest and execution. . . . Dickens devoted a great deal of care to Fagin's
death. He clearly conceived of it not as the just punishment
of a criminal, but as a ritual of exorcism and purification.
The scene is built up symphonically, with noises off from
the carpenters constructing the scaffold, the clock tolling the
hours away, and the cheerful bustle of morning carried on
as if the day were not out of the ordinary. At the centre of the
whole, Fagin, in a terrible loneliness, is gradually disinte-
grating under the pressure. Finally, Oliver comes and sees
him "seated on his bed, rocking himself from side to side,
with a countenance more like that of a snared beast than the
face of a man. His mind was evidently wandering to his old
life, for he continued to mutter, without appearing conscious
of their presence otherwise than as a part of his vision"
(Chapter 52). . . . With this final confrontation of Oliver and
Fagin in the condemned cell, the novel reaches its real conclusion. For it is this confrontation that is at the centre of
everything, like the melodic phrase or harmonic idea at the
heart of a string quartet.

I have dwelt at length upon the dream logic of *Oliver Twist*
and upon the nature of the evil in it, because these qualities
determine each other, and indicate the way Dickens uses the
basic myth at this stage. . . . The story of Oliver's rescue from
destitution and contamination with evil fulfills a deep-
seated need in Dickens (and in many of his contemporaries)
to re-enact, and thereby reaffirm, his emergence from the
abyss of penury and degradation. . . . Dickens is going
through a dreamlike performance here, that expresses a
universal Victorian fear of falling from one class to the one
beneath, and on a broader scale, the universal human fear
of darkness or simply of being lost and corrupted. The true
significance of the performance lies in the nature of the confrontation between good and evil.

# Structure and Theme in *David Copperfield*

T.A. Jackson

T.A. Jackson argues that *David Copperfield* reaches a balance between good and evil, optimism and pessimism. His analysis shows that good events alternate with bad in a plot complicated by numerous subplots. Jackson notes that while bad characters, usually from the upper classes, get their deserved punishment, they often profit, and good characters, usually from the lower classes, suffer in spite of their goodness. T.A. Jackson is the author of *Dialectics: The Logic of Marxism—and Its Critics.*

Broadly speaking, all the characters of wealth and social position [in *Dombey and Son*] turn out to be "bad eggs"; and, with similar reservations, all the characters from the lower orders prove to be "good eggs."

There is, it is true, no clear recognition of class-conflict, as such, and no indication of a function for political struggle. But there is the beginning at any rate of a recognition of class as a positive fact.

A similar conclusion can be drawn from *David Copperfield*. Here the plot is tenuous to non-existence, showing, in fact, an even more complete reversion to the picaresque method—the method of events succeeding events as in a journey of exploration—than do his earlier novels, since it is told in the first person and is in form a quasi-autobiography. If *Oliver Twist* shows most clearly the influence of Smollett, *David Copperfield* shows no less clearly the influence of Defoe.[1] Such plot as there is must, on this method, seem to be fortuitous and extraneous, since the main theme is the arrival of the hero at his self-appointed end—in this case pros-

---

1. George Smollett and Daniel Defoe were eighteenth-century British novelists.

Excerpted from T.A. Jackson, *Charles Dickens: The Progress of a Radical* (New York: International Publishers, 1938). Reprinted by permission of the publisher.

perity and happiness with his second wife, Agnes. . . .

Almost any reader must, in some mood or another find it possible to identify himself with David Copperfield, who might as well, from this standpoint, have been named "Everyman." It is this more or less complete achievement of universality which distinguishes *Copperfield* from all the other novels of Dickens, and marks it out as pivotal in his development. Even less than is the case with *Dombey* can it be said of *Copperfield* that its moral is optimist or pessimist. It is, so far as it is anything, positively meliorist.[2] The total balance of good and evil in the Universe is, on the meliorist view, fixed in sum, since each implies its opposite and any increase in the one implies an increase, actual or potential, in the other. The utmost that human endeavour can achieve is to modify the incidence of the evil in such wise as to insure that avoidable evil is reduced to a minimum. . . .

## THE BALANCE OF GOOD AND EVIL IN THE PLOT

The balance of good and evil, and their mutual interconditioning runs all through the novel. To David's idyllic childhood succeeds his widowed mother's marriage to the vile-natured Mr. Murdstone, who proceeds, under the guise of teaching and "forming David's character" to use the affection of each for the other as a means of torturing both David and his mother. Incidentally also, the occasion of the wedding causes David to begin an acquaintance with the Peggotty household, and with Little Em'ly, which has in the end far-reaching consequences.

David, driven to revolt by Mr. Murdstone's torments, is sent away to the school of the sadistic brute Creakle. Here he is badly treated physically; but, after a time finds the atmosphere much more congenial in that he makes friends with the tearful but buoyant hearted Tommy Traddles, and with the handsome and wilful Steerforth, the spoiled son of a foolish and aristocratic mother. When David's mother dies, crushed under the moral tortures of the Murdstones—brother and sister—David is taken from school, and, child as he is, set to work as a child-labourer in a blacking factory. This infliction has its set-off in that it causes him to make the acquaintance of the inimitable Mr. Micawber, who, however, soon falls into the clutches of his creditors. When Mi-

2. the belief that the world tends to get better and better

cawber, after compounding with his creditors, is forced to remove to Plymouth with his family, David decides to stand it no longer; and sets off to appeal for help to his great-aunt in Dover, Betsy Trotwood—of whom he knows only by repute. Robbed on setting out, he makes his way to Dover on foot. His aunt decides to adopt him; and thereafter he begins a new life. His aunt sends him to a good school, and, his education concluded, gets him articled to a proctor in Doctors' Commons (an ecclesiastical Court nearly all of whose functions have been absorbed by the High Court of Justice).

From this point the main, autobiographical, thread proliferates into a succession of dramatic and melodramatic subplots, each of which would have been, in the hands of almost any other writer, sufficient for an independent novel.

On the main line, so to speak, are David's own love adventures. He falls in love with his employer's daughter, and, after her father's sudden death, marries her. After a brief comedy-idyll of married life the child-wife, Dora, dies. Later on David does what he might have done in the first place, and marries Agnes, the daughter of his aunt's lawyer-agent, Wickfield; and so achieves the "happy ever after" terminus of his adventures.

This final *dénouement is* complicated by the sub-plot of Uriah Heep, a less polished, more hypocritical, and even more villainous Carker. Under a presence of cringing humility, Heep conceals an active malevolence that places him above either Squeers, Quilp, Dennis, Jonas Chuzzlewit, or even Carker in Dickens' list of villains in grain. Heep aspires, on the one hand, to get complete control of his employer's business; and on the other to use that power to force Agnes to marry him. He uses as his means to that end, his employer's weakness for drink; and all but succeeds. He is, however, thwarted, exposed, and forced to disgorge by the detective enterprise of Mr. Micawber, whom he has employed as a clerk—as a means of spying upon David....

## THE NOVEL'S MORAL AMBIGUITY

The moral of *David Copperfield* is elusive. In the main it is expressed in the words of Betsy Trotwood (the best-drawn character in the novel, and the most pleasing) "Never be mean in anything; never be false; never be cruel." But it is apparent from the course of the novel that Dickens has lost his old naive faith that these injunctions alone will ensure peace, prosperity and happiness to all who live their life in their practice. On the contrary: every character in the novel who, tried by this standard, passes muster as "good," is forced to face hardship, disappointment, trial and affliction; and only in the end—and with chastening qualifications— attains to peace, happiness, and a moderate prosperity. It is, on the showing of *David Copperfield,* the good who are forced to suffer most cruelly; and it is their very goodness which provides the means whereby their pain is inflicted. The bad characters, on the other hand, while they, too, are checked and thwarted—and, in the case of Uriah Heep, forced to disgorge their ill-gotten gains—do not, in fact, suffer anything like so much. Steerforth, for instance—who, though a villain, is so, more as a result of a foolish upbringing than by reason of natural wickedness—works mischief far beyond any power of recompense. He suffers, in that he is never happy, is haunted by remorse, and is, in the end, drowned. But he does not suffer anything like so much as does Little Em'ly, or as do her relatives, and David on her account. Steerforth's mother, too, stricken into paralysis and loss of reason, by her son's death, suffers a far more drastic penalty than he.

More telling still on the pessimist side of the account is the fact that, though Uriah Heep does, in the end, land in gaol, he is shown there as swindling still, and still gaining benefits by the exercise of hypocritical presences. Most telling of all is the fact that Murdstone is shown not only as surviving but as practicing profitably on a fresh victim the very deceits and cruelties he had inflicted fatally upon David's mother.

The politico-social moral of *David Copperfield* seems, therefore, to be identical with that of *Dombey and Son.* Life in general is an inexplicable muddle, of which it is possible to make the best or the worst. It is finer and nobler to make the best of it; but such rewards as this course will bring are moral and subjective, only; and even they must be bought with a price.

## DICKENS' ATTITUDES TOWARD THE SOCIAL CLASSES

There is, however, in *Copperfield,* a change in Dickens' class-orientation. The only quasi-aristocratic characters in the book—the Steerforths, and also certain connections of Mrs. Strong, the wife of the benevolent schoolmaster—fall definitely into the "bad" category. The well-to-do bourgeois characters, are, with the exception of Betsy Trotwood—and her amiable, but deranged, companion, Mr. Dick—either scoundrels, as Murdstone is, liars like Mr. Spenlow, or moral weaklings like Mr. Wickfield. It is the lower middle-class and proletarian characters, such as Micawber and Tommy Traddles in the first category, and the whole Peggotty family in the second, who occupy the centre of the stage and reap all the laurels. In fact, the juxtaposition of the Steerforth and Peggotty families issues in something very near to natural class-antagonism—a fact which Dickens himself suggests through the mouth of Steerforth.

When the proposed visit to Yarmouth and the Peggotty family is mooted[3] to Mrs. Steerforth and her companion Rosa Dartle—who, we learn in the end, is secretly Steerforth's discarded mistress (torn continually between infatuation for him, hatred for herself for having been his mistress, and hatred for him for having discarded her, as well as for those who have taken her place) Rosa Dartle asks whether "that sort of people," meaning the Peggotty family, are really "animals and clods, and beings of another order." Steerforth answers in a way that, at the time, David takes to be ironical:

> "Why, there's a pretty wide separation between them and us," said Steerforth with indifference. "They are not to be expected to be as sensitive as we are. Their delicacy is not to be shocked, or hurt very easily. They are wonderfully virtuous, I dare say—some people contend for that, at least, and I am sure I don't want to contradict them—but they have not very fine natures, and they may be thankful that, like their coarse rough skins, they are not easily wounded." (Chap. XX)

In the subsequent working-out of the whole Little Em'ly sub-plot, Steerforth is shown as acting fully in the spirit of this proposition; while every member of the Peggotty household down to and including even Mrs. Gummidge (the "lone, lore, creature," always lamenting "the old 'un," her lost husband), shows each in a different way how revoltingly false it is. The Peggotty household, in fact, contains by far the finest, most delicate, and most sensitive natures to appear in the novel; and the contrast is heightened to the pitch of absolute antagonism when both Mrs. Steerforth and Rosa Dartle, the one with self-centred aristocratic scorn, the other with jealous fury, refuse to believe that any sort of injury, physical,

3. broached

mental or moral, could be inflicted on "that sort of people" which money would not more than compensate.

This class-moral is reinforced by a number of side strokes. One of the most obvious is that given by the casually-introduced character, Mrs. Henry Spiker, the wife of a Treasury solicitor, who "looks like Hamlet's aunt." At a dinner-table she follows the lead of her hostess, Mrs. Waterbrook, and discourses on the Aristocracy and Blood:

> "I confess I am of Mrs. Waterbrook's opinion," said Mr. Waterbrook, with his wine-glass at his eye. " Other things are all very well in their way, but give me Blood!"

> "Oh! There is nothing," observed Hamlet's aunt, "so satisfactory to one! There is nothing that is so much one's *beau idéal*[4] of—of all that sort of thing; speaking generally. There are some low minds (not many I am happy to believe, but there are *some*) that would prefer to do what *I* should call bow down before idols. Positively Idols! Before services, intellect and so on. But these are intangible points. Blood is not so. We see Blood in a nose, and we know it. We meet with it in a chin and we say, 'There it is! That's Blood!' It is an actual matter of fact. We point it out. It admits of no doubt."

> The simpering fellow, with the weak legs, who had taken Agnes down, stated the question more decisively yet, I thought.

> "Oh, you know, deuce take it," said this gentleman, looking round the board with an imbecile smile, "we can't forego Blood, you know. We must have Blood, you know. Some young fellows, you know, may be a little behind their station perhaps in point of education and behaviour, and may go a little wrong, you know, and get themselves and other people into a variety of fixes—and all that—but deuce take it, it's delightful to reflect that they've got Blood in 'em! Myself, I'd rather at any time be knocked down by a man who had got Blood in him, than I'd be picked up by a man who hadn't!"

> This sentiment, as comprising the general question into a nutshell, gave the utmost satisfaction, and brought the gentleman into great notice until the ladies retired. (Chap. XXV)

There is here expressed more than the ordinary bourgeois-Liberal contempt for the aristocracy of Blood and an exaltation, as against it, of the (so-called) aristocracy of talent. The company are none of them aristocrats; hence their deference to "Blood" is manifestly the most contemptible of toadyism. . . .

4. beautiful ideal

## THE OUTSTANDING QUALITIES OF *DAVID COPPERFIELD*

*David Copperfield* is outstanding among Dickens' novels on several grounds. It was his own favourite. It was his first attempt at a novel in the first person; and is, probably in consequence of this, much more genuinely autobiographical than any of his previous—or, for the matter of that, any of his later—novels. His powers had clearly, in *Copperfield*, reached their maximum expansion. His ability to invent a character at a moment's notice is not, perhaps, so obvious as in his earlier work. But it is more definitely under control. His plan undergoes much less modification in progress than did that of *Pickwick*, for instance, or even that of *Dombey*. . . . Dickens' mastery of his chosen medium is shown at its completest in *Copperfield*.

# Mr. Micawber: A Comic Character in *David Copperfield*

J.B. Priestley

J.B. Priestley ranks Mr. Micawber in *David Copperfield* as Dickens's greatest comic character, calling him a fool and a joke. Priestley's examples illustrate the absurd imaginary world Mr. Micawber creates for himself, a world in which he interprets dismal circumstances with utmost optimism. Though Priestley criticizes Dickens's plot, he believes this comic character is more memorable than any story. J.B. Priestley is a novelist, a dramatist, and a critic. He is author of the novel *The Good Companion*, the play *I Have Been There Before*, and a critical work on the life of George Meredith.

[In *David Copperfield*] David is taken into the counting-house and introduced to his new landlord:

> A stoutish, middle-aged person, in a brown surtout¹ and black tights and shoes, with no more hair upon his head (which was a large one, and very shining) than there is upon an egg, and with a very extensive face, which he turned full upon me. His clothes were shabby, but he had an imposing shirt-collar on. He carried a jaunty sort of stick, with a large pair of rusty tassels to it; and a quizzing-glass hung outside his coat,—for ornament, I afterwards found, as he very seldom looked through it, and couldn't see anything when he did.

. . . Mr. Micawber is unquestionably the greatest of all Dickens' comic figures. Unlike so many of the others, he is droll both in character and in speech; he would be vastly entertaining if he were only described to us, if we were only allowed to see him from a distance and never met him face to

---

1. a man's long, close-fitting overcoat

Excerpted from J.B. Priestley, *The English Comic Characters* (London: Bodley Head, 1963). Reprinted by permission of Random House UK Ltd.

face or heard him speak; the idea of him is comic; but in addition to that, of course, he is infinitely droll in speech, always saying the kind of thing we expect him to say but always saying it better, being more himself, so to speak, every time we meet him, as such persons are in real life. He is not only the greatest of Dickens' comic figures, but, with the one exception of Falstaff, he is the greatest comic figure in the whole range of English literature. . . . Micawber must be included in quite another category, namely, that of the great solemn fools, who do not offer us their wit and humour but only themselves, who do not make jokes but are themselves one endless joke. . . .

The story that Micawber adorns is different from the other Dickens novels in having a certain autobiographical basis: Dickens is making direct use of a number of his own childish experiences. There strolled magnificently through all the memories of his childhood and youth one extraordinary figure, his father, John Dickens, and it was he who became Mr. Micawber. . . .

## QUALITIES OF A GREAT COMIC CHARACTER

Micawber, in his talk, has all the wild absurdity of a comic individual, and particularly, of course, a comic Dickens individual, and he has too the psychological richness and solidity of a universal type and is therefore, unlike so many entertaining characters, a fruitful theme for any man's discourse. Volumes passing a score of philosophies under review could be written on the Micawbers.

Really great absurdities of speech are like really great passages of poetry, they cannot be analysed any more than a scent can be analysed; they are simply miraculous assemblages of words. Why they should be so ridiculous is, and must remain, a mystery. Faced with them, we can only enjoy and give thanks, taking our analysis elsewhere. In the last resort, speech and character cannot, of course, be separated, one being the expression of the other, and concerning Mr. Micawber's character there is a great deal to be said. . . .

## MR. MICAWBER LIVES IN HIS OWN IMAGINARY WORLD

The secret of Mr. Micawber is that he does not really live in this world at all: he lives in a world of his own. It is a world in which he himself is clearly a man of talent, for whom great prizes are waiting round the next corner, where an IOU

clearly set out and given to the proper person or an entry in
a little notebook is as good as cash down, where everything
is larger and simpler and richer and more romantic than the
things of this world. In short—to echo him once more—he
lives entirely in his imagination: he has the real artistic temperament. Let circumstances cast him down ever so little,
then he cries farewell and plunges headlong into the dark
gulf of despair; but within a short space of time he has not
only climbed out of that gulf into the common daylight of ordinary cheerfulness, he has soared away into the very
empyrean of human happiness: he will have no half-
measures in his moods, because a robust, romantic, and (to
speak truth) somewhat theatrical imagination takes no delight in half-measures; it demands either the green limelight
and the muted strings or every light in the house ablaze and
the full orchestra crashing in triumph. But the real world,
observing that Wilkins Micawber will not consent to live in
it, plans a hearty revenge. It contrives that the said Micawber
shall be for ever in difficulties; that his talent shall pass un-
recognised (except by Mrs. Micawber) and his offers—as she
herself tells us—received with contumely; that neither corn
nor coals shall sustain him, and that he shall be for ever head
over ears in debt, existing in a wilderness of notes of hand,
discounted bills, and IOU's; and so, eternally jostled by creditors and bailiffs, in and out of the debtors' prison, exchang-
ing one set of miserable lodgings for another, pawning the
few remaining possessions in order to pay for the next meal,
he and his wife and their ever-increasing family are for ever
driven from pillar to post, can never breathe freely, clear
themselves, settle down as decent citizens willing and able to
look any man in the face; and thus would seem to be in a
truly wretched condition. Short of actual crime—and borrowing on such a scale appears to be dangerously near a
criminal proceeding—it is hardly possible to imagine an existence more squalid, uncomfortable, and hopeless. This
world, it would seem, has revenged itself very thoroughly.

But actually it has done nothing of the kind, for Mr. Micawber remains unscathed, living as he does in some other
world of his own. The above account of his way of life is true
enough as it is glimpsed from the real world; but Mr. Micawber himself does not really see it like this, as we may
gather from his talk, nor does his wife, nor, indeed, does any
one who is under the spell of his glamorous imagination and

walks with him for a space in his own private Eden. If a man who has just been quarrelling with the turncock from the waterworks can dismiss the matter with a reference to 'the momentary laceration of a wounded spirit, made sensitive by a recent collision with the Minion of Power,' he is beyond the corroding touch of bitter circumstance; the slings and arrows of outrageous fortune whistle by, leaving him unhurt; his imagination has provided him with one of those fairy cloaks that enable their wearers to brave all dangers. Mr. Micawber sees himself as the central figure in some colossal wild romance, to which even the most disastrous events do but add an intensely absorbing and moving chapter or so and call for nobler attitudes and more magnificent rhetoric on the part of the principal actor. Once things are seen in that romantic haze, so that they loom splendid or sinister and run riot in scarlet and black and gold, the dreariness, the hopelessness, of the petty tale that is the world's report of Mr. Micawber's life completely disappear: he goes his way to the sound of epic drums, the trumpets of tragedy, and the flutes and violins of romance. To him, the present is always a crisis, whether of good or ill fortune matters not, a crisis to be enjoyed as the latest and strangest scene in the drama; the past, far from being a hopeless record from which remembrance turns her face, is an Othello's tale of battles, sieges, fortunes, of moving accidents by flood and field, of hairbreadth 'scapes i' the imminent deadly breach; the future, shining round the next corner, is a happy ending.

## THE CONTRAST BETWEEN THE REAL WORLD AND MR. MICAWBER'S

What chance has poverty, with its poor shifts and wretched limitations, its dinginess and drabness, with a mind so wedded to high romance, so intoxicated with opulent images and phrases, so richly nourished by the milk and honey of words? What does it matter what facts have to be faced if they are first sent to the carnival of the romantic imagination and so always return the strangest and most fascinating company, still moving to music in their tragic and comic masks? David was a poor little fellow of ten, a timid little washer of bottles, when he lodged, dingily and precariously like a mouse, with the Micawbers; but Mr. Micawber, meeting him again after a lapse of years, can drink 'to the days when my friend Copperfield and myself were younger, and fought our way in the world side by side.' On their first meeting again, at Canterbury, when David tells him that he is now at school, he can remark: 'Although a mind like my friend Copperfield's does not require that cultivation which, without his knowledge of men and things, it would require, still it is a rich soil teeming with latent vegetation.' Later, when they meet in the company of Traddles, Mr. Micawber refers to his affairs as a somewhat romantic historian, engaged in the chronicle of the whole world, might refer to the position of some great empire at a crisis in its history:

> 'You find us, Copperfield,' said Mr. Micawber, with one eye on Traddles, 'at present established, on what may be designated as a small and unassuming scale; but, you are aware that I have, in the course of my career, surmounted difficulties, and conquered obstacles. You are no stranger to the fact, that there have been periods of my life, when it has been requisite that I should pause, until certain unexpected events should turn up; when it has been necessary that I should fall back, before making what I trust I shall not be accused of presumption in terming—a spring. The present is one of those momentous stages in the life of a man. You find me, fallen back, *for* a spring; and I have every reason to believe that a vigorous leap will shortly be the result.'

And his subsequent review of the situation, his parting speech, in the manner in which it succeeds in casting a curious glamour over everything, transforming the most trumpery and prosaic matter into something rich and strange, gives us the complete Micawber, soaring high above this world of 'offices and the witness-box':

> 'My dear Copperfield, I need hardly tell you that to have beneath our roof, under existing circumstances, a mind like that which gleams—if I may be allowed the expression—which gleams—in your friend Traddles, is an unspeakable comfort. With a washerwoman, who exposes hard-bake for sale in her parlour-window, dwelling next door, and a Bow-street officer residing over the way, you may imagine that his society is a source of consolation to myself and to Mrs. Micawber. I am at present, my dear Copperfield, engaged in the sale of corn upon commission. It is not an avocation of a remunerative description—in other words, it does *not* pay—and some temporary embarrassments of a pecuniary nature have been the consequence. I am, however, delighted to add that I have now an immediate prospect of something turning up (I am not at liberty to say in what direction), which I trust will enable me to provide, permanently, both for myself and for your friend Traddles, in whom I have an unaffected interest. You may, perhaps, be prepared to hear that Mrs. Micaw-

ber is in a state of health which renders it not wholly improbable that an addition may be ultimately made to those
pledges of affection which—in short, to the infantine group.
Mrs. Micawber's family have been so good as to express their
dissatisfaction at this state of things. I have mercy to observe
that I am not aware it is any business of theirs, and that I
repel that exhibition of feeling with scorn, and with defiance!'

An excellent example of our friend's Front Bench[2] manner, in
which every polysyllabic phrase suggests at least five thousand a year and a substantial pension. What is an empty
pocket compared to such verbal riches? Selling corn upon
commission may be a poor business, but once it is referred to
as 'not an avocation of a remunerative description' it somehow
suggests that immense wealth is lying only just beyond the
speaker's grasp; it takes us immediately into an atmosphere of
prosperity. What is a balance at the bank to a man who has
only to open his mouth to shower riches about him like some
one in a fairy tale, whose very tongue is an alchemist?

Living in the world as he does, not as some poor devil trying to patch together a bare existence and evade his creditors, but as the central and heroic figure in that amazing
chronicle, The Life and Times of Wilkins Micawber, Lover,
Husband, Father, Financier, and Philosopher, Mr. Micawber
instinctively seizes hold of every situation, good or evil, that
presents itself and makes the most of it. Faced with such romantic gusto, so fine an appreciation of a crisis, revelling
even in profound despair and last farewells, ill fortune, try as
it may, can hardly make itself felt. And the commonplace,
that drab stuff which is the fabric of most of our days, van-
ishes entirely: it is hardly conceivable that Mr. Micawber can
ever have had a dull moment. It would be difficult to imagine anything more dreary than the prospect of being a clerk
to a petty solicitor in a small cathedral town, or anything less
exciting and romantic than a family removal from London to
Canterbury; but Mr. Micawber, on the eve of his removal to
Uriah Heep's stands before us as a man who has just seen
Troy burn and is now about to embark on an Odyssey. And
so, of course, he is: it is we who are blind and deaf and spir-
itless in our boredom. 'It may be expected,' the great creature
declares to his friends, 'that on the eve of a migration which
will consign us to a perfectly new existence, I should offer a
few valedictory remarks to two such friends as I see before

2. politicians in the House of Commons

me. But all that I have to say in this way, I have said. Whatever station in society I may attain, through the medium of the learned profession of which I am about to become an unworthy member, I shall endeavour not to disgrace, and Mrs. Micawber will be safe to adorn.' Being able now to cast off his disguise (the name 'Mortimer' and a pair of spectacles—and who can doubt that he enjoyed both immensely?), he speaks as one who has long been an exile or spent half a lifetime in remote hiding-places, and his language leaps up to grapple with the romantic moment: 'The cloud has passed from the dreary scene, and the God of Day is once more high upon the mountain tops. On Monday next, on the arrival of the four o'clock afternoon coach at Canterbury, my foot will be on my native heath—my name, Micawber.'

## THE MICAWBERS MOVE TO AUSTRALIA

No sooner is Australia mentioned ('the land, the only land, for myself and my family'—though he has obviously never given it a thought before) than he sees a new part for himself and plunges into it. Within an hour or so, we are told, he is walking the streets of Canterbury—'expressing, in the hardy roving manner he assumed, the unsettled habits of a temporary sojourner in the land; and looking at the bullocks, as they came by, with the eye of an Australian farmer.' And as the plans for emigration mature, he becomes still more wildly colonial. What could be better than the steps he has taken to familiarise himself and his family with the conditions of Australian life?

> 'My eldest daughter attends at five every morning at a neighbouring establishment, to acquire the process—if process it may be called—of milking cows. My younger children are instructed to observe, as closely as circumstances will permit, the habits of the pigs and poultry maintained in the poorer parts of this city: a pursuit from which they have, on two occasions, been brought home, within an inch of being run over. I have myself directed some attention, during the past week, to the art of baking; and my son Wilkins has issued forth with a walking-stick and driven cattle, when permitted, by the rugged hirelings who had them in charge, to render any voluntary service in that direction—which I regret to say, for the credit of our nature, was not often; he being generally warned, with imprecations, to desist.'

Once on board the ship, he combines, with great skill, both the colonial and nautical characters. With a low-crowned straw hat, a complete suit of oilskins, a telescope, and a trick of 'casting up his eye at the sky as looking out for dirty weather,' he is nothing less than an old salt, and we can be sure that he carried out his intention of spinning an occasional yarn before the galley-fire. . . .

Happy Mr. Micawber, joyously combining the rôles of financier, sailor, and pioneer, but, in truth, only travelling in a dream, from an England that was never there to an Australia that he will invent, sailing from moonshine to moonshine. . . .

## MR. MICAWBER'S ROLE IN THE NOVEL

Nothing has been said so far about the part that Mr. Micawber is made to play in the story, a part that has been severely criticised, not least by his greatest admirers. Of the emigration and Mr. Micawber's purely material success at the end of the story, Mr. G.K. Chesterton has remarked: 'But how did it happen that the man who created this Micawber could pension him off at the end of the story and make him a successful colonial mayor?'. . . If it is simply regarded as a new setting for Mr. Micawber, giving him, as it were, more scope for his Micawberishness, then it can be justified. . . .

But of his part as a detective in the history of David Copperfield it is impossible to put forward any defence. It is impossible to read those chapters without feeling that Micawber is being constrained by his creator: even the humour is forced and unreal. . . . This trick of hurling his great drolls into the plot of the story and compelling them to play some quite unlikely part is, of course, one of the most notable defects in Dickens. . . . But Dickens, an extremely conscientious author, thought that the characters existed for the sake of the stories. . . . This was only the view of the conventional author, the superficial Dickens; the real man knew better and, in his heart of hearts, realised that these great comic figures of his were their own excuse and needed no complicated intrigue to justify their existence. . . .

There is only one thing better than a story, and that is—a character. A character is half-a-hundred stories at once, the source of endless fables; and it is something more, particularly if it is a comic character. . . . The humour of incident and situation that does not proceed from character, however artfully it may be contrived, is at its best only an elaborate play, making a glitter and commotion on the surface of things. But the humour of character goes down and touches, surely but tenderly, the very roots of our common human nature.

# CHAPTER 4

# Novels of Reform, History, and Morality

READINGS ON
CHARLES DICKENS

# Social Criticism in *Hard Times*

George Bernard Shaw

George Bernard Shaw argues that *Hard Times* reflects Dickens's shift from individual heroes and villains to criticism of society as a whole, and that Coketown symbolizes the evils of industrial England in the 1850s—the destruction of the environment and the exploitation of workers. To enjoy this novel in contrast to Dickens's earlier novels, Shaw maintains that readers must view characters differently and find new forms of humor. George Bernard Shaw was a famous Victorian playwright who wrote more than a dozen plays, among them *Man and Superman, Pygmalion,* and *Saint Joan.*

John Ruskin[1] once declared *Hard Times* Dickens's best novel. It is worth while asking why Ruskin thought this, because he would have been the first to admit that the habit of placing works of art in competition with one another, and wrangling as to which is the best, is the habit of the sportsman, not of the enlightened judge of art. Let us take it that what Ruskin meant was that *Hard Times* was one of his special favorites among Dickens's books. Was this the caprice of fancy? or is there any rational explanation of the preference? I think there is.

*Hard Times* is the first fruit of that very interesting occurrence which our religious sects call, sometimes conversion, sometimes being saved, sometimes attaining to conviction of sin. Now the great conversions of the XIX century were not convictions of individual, but of social sin. The first half of the XIX century considered itself the greatest of all the centuries. The second discovered that it was the wickedest of all

1. British essayist

Excerpted from George Bernard Shaw's Introduction to *Hard Times* by Charles Dickens (London, 1912).

the centuries. The first half despised and pitied the Middle Ages as barbarous, cruel, superstitious, ignorant. The second half saw no hope for mankind except in the recovery of the faith, the art, the humanity of the Middle Ages....

*Hard Times* was written in 1854, just at the turn of the half century; and in it we see Dickens with his eyes newly open and his conscience newly stricken by the discovery of the real state of England. In the book that went immediately before, *Bleak House,* he was still denouncing evils and ridiculing absurdities that were mere symptoms of the anarchy that followed the industrial revolution of the XVIII and XIX centuries, and the conquest of political power by Commercialism in 1832. In *Bleak House* Dickens knows nothing of the industrial revolution: he imagines that what is wrong is that when a dispute arises over the division of the plunder of the nation, the Court of Chancery, instead of settling the dispute cheaply and promptly, beggars the disputants and pockets both their shares....

## DICKENS'S NEW SOCIAL CRITICISM

In *Hard Times* you will find all this changed. Coketown, which you can see to-day for yourself in all its grime in the Potteries (the real name of it is Hanley in Staffordshire on the London and North Western Railway), is not, like Tom All Alone's, a patch of slum in a fine city, easily cleared away, as Tom's actually was about fifty years after Dickens called attention to it. Coketown is the whole place; and its rich manufacturers are proud of its dirt, and declare that they like to see the sun blacked out with smoke, because it means that the furnaces are busy and money is being made; whilst its poor factory hands have never known any other sort of town, and are as content with it as a rat is with a hole. Mr. Rouncewell, the pillar of society who snubs Sir Leicester with such dignity, has become Mr. Bounderby, the self-made humbug. The Chancery suitors who are driving themselves mad by hanging about the Courts in the hope of getting a judgment in their favor instead of trying to earn an honest living, are replaced by factory operatives who toil miserably and incessantly only to see the streams of gold they set flowing slip through their fingers into the pockets of men who revile and oppress them.

Clearly this is not the Dickens who burlesqued the old song of the Fine Old English Gentleman, and saw in the evils he attacked only the sins and wickednesses and follies of a great civilization. This is Karl Marx, Thomas Carlyle, Ruskin, William Morris, Edward Carpenter,[2] rising up against civilization itself as against a disease, and declaring that it is not our disorder but our order that is horrible; that it is not our criminals but our magnates that are robbing and murdering us; and that it is not merely Tom All Alone's that must be demolished and abolished, pulled down, rooted up, and made for ever impossible so that nothing shall remain of it but History's record of its infamy, but our entire social system. . . .

In short, whereas formerly men said to the victim of society who ventured to complain, "Go and reform yourself before you pretend to reform Society," it now has to admit that until Society is reformed, no man can reform himself except in the most insignificantly small ways. He may cease picking your pocket of half crowns; but he cannot cease taking a quarter of a million a year from the community for nothing at one end of the scale, or living under conditions in which health, decency, and gentleness are impossible at the other, if he happens to be born to such a lot.

You must therefore resign yourself, if you are reading Dickens's books in the order in which they were written, to bid adieu now to the light-hearted and only occasionally indignant Dickens of the earlier books, and get such entertainment as you can from him now that the occasional indignation has spread and deepened into a passionate revolt against the whole industrial order of the modern world. Here you will find no more villains and heroes, but only oppressors and victims, oppressing and suffering in spite of themselves, driven by a huge machinery which grinds to pieces the people it should nourish and ennoble, and having for its directors the basest and most foolish of us instead of the noblest and most farsighted.

## READERS' REACTIONS TO *HARD TIMES*

Many readers find the change disappointing. Others find Dickens worth reading almost for the first time. The increase in strength and intensity is enormous: the power that indicts a nation so terribly is much more impressive than that which ridicules individuals. But it cannot be said that there is an increase of simple pleasure for the reader,

2. essayists and social reformers

though the books are not therefore less attractive. One cannot say that it is pleasanter to look at a battle than at a merry-go-round; but there can be no question which draws the larger crowd.

To describe the change in the readers' feelings more precisely, one may say that it is impossible to enjoy Gradgrind or Bounderby as one enjoys Pecksniff or the Artful Dodger or Mrs. Gamp or Micawber or Dick Swiveller, because these earlier characters have nothing to do with us except to amuse us. We neither hate nor fear them. We do not expect ever to meet them, and should not be in the least afraid of them if we did. England is not full of Micawbers and Swivellers. They are not our fathers, our schoolmasters, our employers, our tyrants. We do not read novels to escape from them and forget them: quite the contrary. But England is full of Bounderbys and Podsnaps and Gradgrinds; and we are all to a quite appalling extent in their power. We either hate and fear them or else we are them, and resent being held up to odium by a novelist. We have only to turn to the article on Dickens in the current edition of the *Encyclopedia Britannica* to find how desperately our able critics still exalt all Dickens's early stories about individuals whilst ignoring or belittling such masterpieces as *Hard Times, Little Dorrit, Our Mutual Friend,* and even *Bleak House* (because of Sir Leicester Dedlock), for their mercilessly faithful and penetrating exposures of English social, industrial, and political life; to see how hard Dickens hits the conscience of the governing class; and how loth we still are to confess, not that we are so wicked (for of that we are rather proud), but so ridiculous, so futile, so incapable of making our country really prosperous. *The Old Curiosity Shop* was written to amuse you, entertain you, touch you; and it succeeded. *Hard Times* was written to make you uncomfortable; and it will make you uncomfortable (and serve you right) though it will perhaps interest you more, and certainly leave a deeper scar on you, than any two of its forerunners.

At the same time you need not fear to find Dickens losing his good humor and sense of fun and becoming serious in Mr. Gradgrind's way. On the contrary, Dickens in this book casts off, and casts off for ever, all restraint on his wild sense of humor. . . .

Mrs. Sparsit in this book, though Rembrandt could not have drawn a certain type of real woman more precisely to the life, is grotesque from beginning to end in her way of expressing herself. Her nature, her tricks of manner, her way of taking Mr. Bounderby's marriage, her instinct for hunting down Louisa and Mrs. Pegler, are drawn with an unerring hand; and she says nothing that is out of character. But no clown gone suddenly mad in a very mad harlequinade could express all these truths in more extravagantly ridiculous speeches. Dickens's business in life has become too serious for troubling over the small change of verisimilitude, and denying himself and his readers the indulgence of his humor in inessentials. He even calls the schoolmaster Mc-Choakumchild, which is almost an insult to the serious reader. And it was so afterwards to the end of his life. There are moments when he imperils the whole effect of his character drawing by some overpoweringly comic sally. For instance, happening in *Hard Times* to describe Mr. Bounderby as drumming on his hat as if it were a tambourine, which is quite correct and natural, he presently says that "Mr. Bounderby put his tambourine on his head, like an oriental dancer." Which similitude is so unexpectedly and excruciatingly funny that it is almost impossible to feel duly angry with the odious Bounderby afterwards.

This disregard of naturalness in speech is extraordinarily entertaining in the comic method; but it must be admitted that it is not only not entertaining, but sometimes hardly bearable when it does not make us laugh. There are two persons in *Hard Times*, Louisa Gradgrind and Cissy Jupe, who are serious throughout. Louisa is a figure of poetic tragedy; and there is no question of naturalness in her case: she speaks from beginning to end as an inspired prophetess, conscious of her own doom and finally bearing to her father the judgment of Providence on his blind conceit. If you once consent to overlook her marriage, which is none the less an act of prostitution because she does it to obtain advantages for her brother and not for herself, there is nothing in the solemn poetry of her deadly speech that jars. But Cissy is nothing if not natural; and though Cissy is as true to nature in her character as Mrs. Sparsit, she "speaks like a book" in the most intolerable sense of the words. In her interview with Mr. James Harthouse, her unconscious courage and simplicity, and his hopeless defeat by them, are quite natural and right; and the contrast between the humble girl of the people and the smart sarcastic man of the world whom she so completely vanquishes is excellently dramatic. . . .

There is, however, one real failure in the book. Slack-bridge, the trade union organizer, is a mere figment of the middle-class imagination. No such man would be listened to by a meeting of English factory hands. . . . We cannot say that Dickens did not know the working classes, because he knew humanity too well to be ignorant of any class. But this sort of knowledge is as compatible with ignorance of class manners and customs as with ignorance of foreign languages. Dickens knew certain classes of working folk very well: domestic servants, village artisans, and employees of petty tradesmen, for example. But of the segregated factory populations of our purely industrial towns he knew no more than an observant professional man can pick up on a flying visit to Manchester.

## DICKENS'S ATTITUDE TOWARD TRADE UNIONS

It is especially important to notice that Dickens expressly says in this book that the workers were wrong to organize themselves in trade unions, thereby endorsing what was perhaps the only practical mistake of the Gradgrind school that really mattered much. . . . Here is a significant passage.

> "Now perhaps," said Mr. Bounderby, "you will let the gentleman know how you would set this muddle (as you are so fond of calling it) to rights."

> "I donno, sir. I canna be expecten to't. Tis not me as should be looken to for that, sir. Tis they as is put ower me, and ower aw the rest of us. What do they tak upon themseln, sir, if not to do it?"

And to this Dickens sticks for the rest of his life. In *Our Mutual Friend* he appeals again and again to the governing classes, asking them with every device of reproach, invective, sarcasm, and ridicule of which he is master, what they have to say to this or that evil which it is their professed business to amend or avoid. Nowhere does he appeal to the working classes to take their fate into their own hands and try the democratic plan.

# Harsh Truth in *Hard Times*

G.K. Chesterton

G.K. Chesterton argues that *Hard Times* is best seen in the context of British history following the American and French Revolutions. In this context, Chesterton argues, Dickens alone notices that the British championed liberty but neglected equality and fraternity, the other two ideals of the French Revolution. *Hard Times* exposes inequality and the wide gap between the rich and the poor that resulted from the exploitation of workers during nineteenth-century industrialization. G.K. Chesterton was a British essayist, critic, novelist, and poet who published in all of those forms. He is the author of a biography of Dickens and collections of essays entitled *Heretics, Generally Speaking*, and *What's Wrong with the World*.

I have heard that in some debating clubs there is a rule that the members may discuss anything except religion and politics. I cannot imagine what they do discuss; but it is quite evident that they have ruled out the only two subjects which are either important or amusing. The thing is a part of a certain modern tendency to avoid things because they lead to warmth; whereas, obviously, we ought, even in a social sense, to seek those things specially. The warmth of the discussion is as much a part of hospitality as the warmth of the fire. And it is singularly suggestive that in English literature the two things have died together. The very people who would blame Dickens for his sentimental hospitality are the very people who would also blame him for his narrow political conviction. The very people who would blame him for his narrow radicalism are those who would blame him for his broad fireside. Real conviction and real charity are much nearer than people suppose. Dickens was capable of loving

From G.K. Chesterton's Introduction to *Hard Times* by Charles Dickens (London: J.M. Dent, 1907).

all men; but he refused to love all opinions. The modern humanitarian can love all opinions, but he cannot love all men; he seems, sometimes, in the ecstasy of his humanitarianism, even to hate them all. He can love all opinions, including the opinion that men are unlovable.

## DICKENS AS A FIGHTER WITH CLEAR CONVICTIONS

In feeling Dickens as a lover we must never forget him as a fighter, and a fighter for a creed: but indeed there is no other kind of fighter. The geniality which he spread over all his creations was geniality spread from one centre, from one flaming peak. He was willing to excuse Mr. Micawber for being extravagant; but Dickens and Dickens's doctrine were strictly to decide how far he was to be excused. He was willing to like Mr. Twemlow in spite of his snobbishness, but Dickens and Dickens's doctrine were alone to be judges of how far he was snobbish. There was never a more didactic writer: hence there was never one more amusing. He had no mean modern notion of keeping the moral doubtful. He would have regarded this as a mere piece of slovenliness, like leaving the last page illegible.

Everywhere in Dickens's work these angles of his absolute opinion stood up out of the confusion of his general kindness, just as sharp and splintered peaks stand up out of the soft confusion of the forests. Dickens is always generous, he is generally kind-hearted, he is often sentimental, he is sometimes intolerably maudlin; but you never know when you will not come upon one of the convictions of Dickens; and when you do come upon it you do know it. It is as hard and as high as any precipice or peak of the mountains. The highest and hardest of these peaks is "Hard Times."

It is here more than anywhere else that the sternness of Dickens emerges as separate from his softness; it is here, most obviously, so to speak, that his bones stick out. There are indeed many other books of his which are written better and written in a sadder tone. " Great Expectations" is melancholy in a sense; but it is doubtful of everything, even of its own melancholy. "A Tale of Two Cities" is a great tragedy, but it is still a sentimental tragedy. It is a great drama, but it is still a melodrama. But this tale of "Hard Times" is in some way harsher than all these. For it is the expression of a righteous indignation which cannot condescend to humour and which cannot even condescend to pathos. Twenty times we have taken Dickens's hand and it has been sometimes hot with revelry and sometimes weak with weariness; but this time we start a little, for it is inhumanly cold, and then we realise that we have touched his gauntlet of steel.

## "HARD TIMES" IN THE CONTEXT OF HISTORY

One cannot express the real value of this book without being irrelevant. It is true that one cannot express the real value of anything without being irrelevant. If we take a thing frivolously we can take it separately, but the moment we take a thing seriously, if it were only an old umbrella, it is obvious that that umbrella opens above us into the immensity of the whole universe. But there are rather particular reasons why the value of the book called "Hard Times" should be referred back to great historic and theoretic matters with which it may appear superficially to have little or nothing to do. The chief reason can perhaps be stated thus—that English politics had for more than a hundred years been getting into more and more of a hopeless tangle (a tangle which, of course, has since become even worse), and that Dickens did in some extraordinary way see what was wrong, even if he did not see what was right.

The Liberalism which Dickens and nearly all of his contemporaries professed had begun in the American and the French Revolutions. Almost all modern English criticism upon those revolutions has been vitiated by the assumption that those revolutions burst upon a world which was unprepared for their ideas—a world ignorant of the possibility of such ideas. Somewhat the same mistake is made by those who suggest that Christianity was adopted by a world incapable of criticising it; whereas obviously it was adopted by a world that was tired of criticising everything. The vital mistake that is made about the French Revolution is merely this—that every one talks about it as the introduction of a new idea. It was not the introduction of a new idea; there are no new ideas. Or if there are new ideas, they would not cause the least irritation if they were introduced into political society; because the world having never got used to them there would be no mass of men ready to fight for them at a moment's notice. That which was irritating about the French Revolution was this—that it was not the introduction of a new ideal, but the practical fulfilment of an old one. From the time of the first fairy tales men had always believed ideally in equality, they had always thought that something ought to be done, if anything could be done to redress the balance between Cinderella and the ugly sisters. The irritating thing about the French was not that they said this ought to be done; everybody said that. The irritating thing about the French was that they did it. They proposed to carry out into a positive scheme what had been the vision of humanity; and humanity was naturally annoyed. The kings of Europe did not make war upon the Revolution because it was a blasphemy, but because it was a copy-book maxim which had been just too accurately copied. It was a platitude which they had always held in theory unexpectedly put into practice. The tyrants did not hate democracy because it was a paradox; they hated it because it was a truism which seemed in some danger of coming true.

### THE EFFECT OF THE REVOLUTION ON ENGLISH POLITICS

Now it happens to be hugely important to have this right view of the Revolution in considering its political effects upon England. For the English, being a deeply and indeed excessively romantic people, could never be quite content with this quality of cold and bald obviousness about the republican formula. The republican formula was merely this—that the State must consist of its citizens ruling equally, however unequally they may do anything else. In their capacity of members of the State they are all equally interested in its preservation. But the English soon began to be romantically restless about this eternal truism; they were perpetually trying to turn it into something else, into something more picturesque—progress perhaps, or anarchy. At last they turned it into the highly exciting and highly unsound system of politics, which was known as the Manchester School, and which was expressed with a sort of logical flightiness, more excusable in literature, by Mr. Herbert Spencer.[1] Of course Danton or Washington[2] or any of the original republicans would have thought these people were mad; they would never have admitted for a moment that the State must not interfere with commerce or competition; they would merely have insisted that if the State did interfere, it must really be the State—that is, the whole people. But the distance between the common sense of Danton and

1. philosopher and writer    2. Jacques Danton was a statesman of the French Revolution, George Washington of the American Revolution.

the mere ecstasy of Herbert Spencer marks the English way of colouring and altering the revolutionary idea. The English people as a body went blind, as the saying is, for interpreting democracy entirely in terms of liberty. They said in substance that if they had more and more liberty it did not matter whether they had any equality or any fraternity. But this was violating the sacred trinity of true politics; they confounded the persons and they divided the substance.

Now the really odd thing about England in the nineteenth century is this—that there was one Englishman who happened to keep his head. The men who lost their heads lost highly scientific and philosophical heads; they were great cosmic systematisers like Spencer, great social philosophers like Jeremy Bentham, great practical politicians like Bright, great political economists like John Stuart Mill. The man who kept his head kept a head full of fantastic nonsense; he was a writer of rowdy farces, a demagogue of fiction, a man without education in any serious sense whatever, a man whose whole business was to turn ordinary cockneys into extraordinary caricatures. Yet when all these other children of the Revolution went wrong he, by a mystical something in his bones, went right. He knew nothing of the Revolution; yet he struck the note of it. He returned to the original sentimental commonplace upon which it is forever founded, as the Church is founded on a rock. In an England gone mad about a minor theory he reasserted the original idea—the idea that no one in the State must be too weak to influence the State.

## ONLY DICKENS SAW THE ENTIRE MEANING OF THE REVOLUTION

This man was Dickens. He did this work much more genuinely than it was done by Carlyle or Ruskin;[3] for they were simply Tories making out a romantic case for the return of Toryism. But Dickens was a real Liberal demanding the return of real Liberalism. Dickens was there to remind people that England had rubbed out two words of the revolutionary motto, had left only Liberty and destroyed Equality and Fraternity. In this book, "Hard Times," he specially champions equality. In all his books he champions fraternity.

The atmosphere of this book and what it stands for can be very adequately conveyed in the note on the book by Lord

3. British essayists Thomas Carlyle and John Ruskin

## FACTORY CONDITIONS IN COKETOWN

*In a chapter in* Hard Times *entitled "No Way Out," Dickens describes Coketown and the mill in which Stephen Black-pool and other poor workers labor for the profits of Bounderby.*

The Fairy palaces burst into illumination, before pale morning showed the monstrous serpents of smoke trailing themselves over Coketown. A clattering of clogs upon the pavement; a rapid ringing of bells; and all the melancholy mad elephants, polished and oiled up for the day's monotony, were at their heavy exercise again.

Stephen bent over his loom, quiet, watchful, and steady. A special contrast, as every man was in the forest of looms where Stephen worked, to the crashing, smashing, tearing, piece of mechanism at which he laboured. Never fear, good people of an anxious turn of mind, that Art will consign Nature to oblivion. Set anywhere, side by side, the work of God and the work of man; and the former, even though it be a troop of Hands of very small account, will gain in dignity from the comparison.

So many hundred Hands in this Mill; so many hundred horse Steam Power. It is known, to the force of a single pound weight, what the engine will do; but, not all the calculators of the National Debt can tell me the capacity for good or evil, for love or hatred, for patriotism or discontent, for the decomposition of virtue into vice, or the reverse, at any single moment

---

Macaulay,[4] who may stand as a very good example of the spirit of England in those years of eager emancipation and expanding wealth—the years in which Liberalism was turned from an omnipotent truth to a weak scientific system. Macaulay's private comment on "Hard Times" runs, "One or two passages of exquisite pathos and the rest sullen Socialism." That is not an unfair and certainly not a specially hostile criticism, but it exactly shows how the book struck those people who were mad on political liberty and dead about everything else. Macaulay mistook for a new formula called Socialism what was, in truth, only the old formula called political democracy. He and his Whigs had so thoroughly mauled and modified the original idea of Jean-Jacques Rousseau or Thomas Jefferson that when they saw it again they positively thought that it was something quite new and

4. British essayist Thomas

in the soul of one of these its quiet servants, with the composed faces and the regulated actions. There is no mystery in
it; there is an unfathomable mystery in the meanest of them,
for ever.—Supposing we were to reverse our arithmetic for
material objects, and to govern these awful unknown quanti-
ties by other means!

The day grew strong, and showed itself outside, even
against the flaming lights within. The lights were turned out,
and the work went on. The rain fell, and the Smoke-serpents,
submissive to the curse of all that tribe, trailed themselves
upon the earth. In the waste yard outside, the steam from the
escape pipe, the litter of barrels and old iron, the shining
heaps of coals, the ashes everywhere, were shrouded in a veil
of mist and rain.

The work went on, until the noon-bell rang. More clattering
upon the pavements. The looms, and wheels, and Hands all
out of gear for an hour.

Stephen came out of the hot mill into the damp wind and cold
wet streets, haggard and worn. He turned from his own class
and his own quarter, taking nothing but a little bread as he
walked along, towards the hill on which his principal employer
lived, in a red house with black outside shutters, green inside
blinds, a black street door, up two white steps, Bounderby (in
letters very like himself) upon a brazen plate, and a round
brazen door-handle underneath it, like a brazen full-stop.

Mr. Bounderby was at his lunch.

eccentric. But the truth was that Dickens was not a Socialist,
but an unspoilt Liberal; he was not sullen; nay, rather, he
had remained strangely hopeful. They called him a sullen
Socialist only to disguise their astonishment at finding still
loose about the London streets a happy republican.

Dickens is the one living link between the old kindness
and the new, between the goodwill of the past and the good
works of the future. He links May Day with Bank Holiday,
and he does it almost alone. All the men around him, great
and good as they were, were in comparison puritanical, and
never so puritanical as when they were also atheistic. He is
a sort of solitary pipe down which pours to the twentieth
century the original river of Merry England. And although
this "Hard Times" is, as its name implies, the hardest of his
works, although there is less in it perhaps than in any of the
others of the *abandon* and the buffoonery of Dickens, this
only emphasises the more clearly the fact that he stood al-

most alone for a more humane and hilarious view of democracy. None of his great and much more highly-educated contemporaries could help him in this. Carlyle was as gloomy on the one side as Herbert Spencer on the other. He protested against the commercial oppression simply and solely because it was not only an oppression but a depression. And this protest of his was made specially in the case of the book before us. It may be bitter, but it was a protest against bitterness. It may be dark, but it is the darkness of the subject and not of the author. He is by his own account dealing with hard times, but not with a hard eternity, not with a hard philosophy of the universe. Nevertheless, this is the one place in his work where he does not make us remember human happiness by example as well as by precept. This is, as I have said, not the saddest, but certainly the harshest of his stories. It is perhaps the only place where Dickens, in defending happiness, for a moment forgets to be happy.

## "HARD TIMES": A HARSH VIEW OF SOCIETY

He describes Bounderby and Gradgrind with a degree of grimness and sombre hatred very different from the half-affectionate derision which he directed against the old tyrants or humbugs of the earlier nineteenth century—the pompous Dedlock or the fatuous Nupkins, the grotesque Bumble or the inane Tigg. In those old books his very abuse was benignant; in "Hard Times" even his sympathy is hard. And the reason is again to be found in the political facts of the century. Dickens could be half genial with the older generation of oppressors because it was a dying generation. It was evident, or at least it seemed evident then, that Nupkins could not go on much longer making up the law of England to suit himself; that Sir Leicester Dedlock could not go on much longer being kind to his tenants as if they were dogs and cats. And some of these evils the nineteenth century did really eliminate or improve. For the first half of the century Dickens and all his friends were justified in feeling that the chains were falling from mankind. At any rate, the chains did fall from Mr. Rouncewell the Iron-master. And when they fell from him he picked them up and put them upon the poor.

# A Tale of Two Cities: An Appealing but Flawed Novel

John Gross

John Gross gives a mixed assessment of *A Tale of Two Cities.* He analyzes it as a work with two heroes, neither of whom provides the story with its central force. Gross criticizes Dickens's lack of humor, his thin portrayal of society, and his artificial plot. Yet, readers continue to find pleasure in the novel because, as Gross maintains, the quality of the writing is outstanding. John Gross has taught at the University of London and Cambridge University. He has served on the editorial staff of the *New York Times Book Review* and is the author of *James Joyce* and the editor of *The Age of Kipling* and *The Oxford Book of Essays.*

*A Tale of Two Cities* ends fairly cheerfully with its hero getting killed. . . .

*A Tale of Two Cities* is a tale of two heroes. The theme of the double has such obvious attractions for a writer preoccupied with disguises, rival impulses, and hidden affinities that it is surprising that Dickens didn't make more use of it elsewhere. But no one could claim that his handling of the device is very successful here, or that he has managed to range the significant forces of the novel behind Carton and Darnay. Darnay is, so to speak, the accredited representative of Dickens in the novel, the 'normal' hero for whom a happy ending is still possible. It has been noted, interestingly enough, that he shares his creator's initials—and that is pretty well the only interesting thing about him. Otherwise he is a pasteboard character, completely undeveloped. His position as an exile, his struggles as a language-teacher, his admiration for George Washington are so many openings thrown away.

Excerpted from John Gross, "*A Tale of Two Cities,*" in *Dickens and the Twentieth Century* (Toronto: University of Toronto Press/Routledge & Kegan Paul, 1962). Reprinted by permission of Routledge.

Carton, of course, is a far more striking figure. He belongs to the line of cultivated wastrels who play an increasingly large part in Dickens's novels during the second half of his career, culminating in Eugene Wrayburn; his clearest predecessor, as his name indicates, is the luckless Richard Carstone of *Bleak House*. He has squandered his gifts and drunk away his early promise; his will is broken, but his intellect is unimpaired. In a sense, his opposite is not Darnay at all, but the aggressive Stryver, who makes a fortune by picking his brains. Yet there is something hollow about his complete resignation to failure; his self-abasement in front of Lucie, for instance. ('I am like one who died young . . . I know very well that you can have no tenderness for me . . .') For, stagy a figure though he is, Carton does suggest what Thomas Hardy calls 'fearful unfulfilments'; he still has vitality, and it is hard to believe that he has gone down without a struggle. The total effect is one of energy held unnaturally in check: the bottled-up frustration which Carton represents must spill over somewhere.

## THE FATES OF CARTON AND DARNAY

Carton's and Darnay's fates are entwined from their first meeting, at the Old Bailey trial. Over the dock there hangs a mirror: 'crowds of the wicked and the wretched had been reflected in it, and had passed from its surface and this earth's together. Haunted in a most ghastly manner that abominable place would have been, if the glass could ever have rendered back its reflections, as the ocean is one day to give up its dead' (bk. II, ch. 2). After Darnay's acquittal we leave him with Carton, 'so like each other in feature, so unlike in manner, both reflected in the glass above them'. Reflections, like ghosts, suggest unreality and self-division, and at the end of the same day Carton stares at his own image in the glass and upbraids it: 'Why should you particularly like a man who resembles you? There is nothing in you to like: you know that. Ah, confound you! . . . Come on, and have it out in plain words! You hate the fellow' (bk. II, ch. 4). In front of the mirror, Carton thinks of changing places with Darnay; at the end of the book, he is to take the other's death upon him. Dickens prepares the ground: when Darnay is in jail, it is Carton who strikes Mr Lorry as having 'the wasted air of a prisoner', and when he is visited by Carton on the rescue attempt, he thinks at first that he is 'an apparition of his own imagining'. But Dickens is determined to stick by Darnay: a happy ending *must* be possible. As Lorry and his party gallop to safety with the drugged Darnay, there is an abrupt switch to the first person: 'The wind is rushing after us, and the clouds are flying after us, and the moon is plunging after us, and the whole wild night is in pursuit of us; but so far, we are pursued by nothing else' (bk. III, ch. 13). *We* can make our escape, however narrowly; Carton, expelled from our system, must be abandoned to his fate. . . .

Drained of the will to live, he is shown in the closing chapters of the book as a man courting death, and embracing it when it comes. 'In seasons of pestilence, some of us will have a secret attraction to the disease—a terrible passing inclination to die of it. And all of us have like wonders hidden in our breasts, only needing circumstances to evoke them' (bk. III, ch. 6). It is Carton rather than Darnay who is 'drawn to the loadstone rock'. On his last walk around Paris, a passage which Shaw[1] cites in the preface to *Man and Superman* as proof of Dickens's essentially irreligious nature, his thoughts run on religion: 'I am the Resurrection and the Life.' But his impressions are all of death: the day comes coldly, 'looking like a dead face out of the sky', while on the river 'a trading boat, with a sail of the softened colour of a dead leaf, then glided into his view, floated by him, and died away' (bk. III, ch. 9). His walk recalls an earlier night, when he wandered round London with 'wreaths of dust spinning round and round before the morning blast, as if the desert sand had risen far away and the first spray of it in its advance had begun to overwhelm the city' (bk. II, ch. 5). Then with the wilderness bringing home to him a sense of the wasted powers within him, he saw a momentary mirage of what he might have achieved and was reduced to tears; but now that the city has been overwhelmed in earnest, he is past thinking of what might have been. 'It is a far, far better thing that I do, than I have ever done'—but the 'better thing' might just as well be committing suicide as laying down his life for Darnay. At any rate, he thinks of himself as going towards rest, not towards resurrection. . . .

Still, *A Tale of Two Cities* is not a private nightmare, but a work which continues to give pleasure. Dickens's drives and conflicts are his raw material, not the source of his artistic

1. playwright George Bernard

power, and in itself the fact that the novel twists the French Revolution into a highly personal fantasy proves nothing: so, after all, does *The Scarlet Pimpernel.* Everything depends on the quality of the writing—which is usually one's cue, in talking about Dickens, to pay tribute to his exuberance and fertility. Dickens's genius inheres in minute particulars; later we may discern patterns of symbolism and imagery, a design which lies deeper than the plot, but first we are struck by the lavish heaping-up of acute observations, startling similes, descriptive flourishes, circumstantial embroidery. Or such is the case with every Dickens novel except for the *Tale,* which is written in a style so grey and unadorned that many readers are reluctant to grant it a place in the Canon at all. Dickens wouldn't be Dickens if there weren't occasional touches like the 'hospital procession of negro cupids, several headless and all cripples', which Mr Lorry notices framing the mirror in his hotel (or the whitewashed cupid 'in the coolest linen' on the ceiling of his Paris office, which makes its appearance three hundred pages later). But for the most part one goes to the book for qualities which are easier to praise than to illustrate or examine: a rapid tempo which never lets up from the opening sentence, and a sombre eloquence which saves Carton from mere melodrama....

## THE NOVEL'S FAULTS

But it must be admitted that the *Tale* is in many ways a thin and uncharacteristic work, bringing the mounting despair of the 1850s to a dead end rather than ushering in the triumphs of the sixties. In no other novel, not even *Hard Times,* has Dickens's natural profusion been so drastically pruned. Above all, the book is notoriously deficient in humour....

Contrary to what might be expected, this absence of burlesque is accompanied by a failure to present society in any depth: *A Tale of Two Cities* may deal with great political events, but nowhere else in the later work of Dickens is there less sense of society as a living organism. Evrémondes and Defarges alike seem animated by sheer hatred; we hear very little of the stock social themes, money, hypocrisy, and snobbery....

The lack of social density shows up Dickens's melodrama to disadvantage. This is partly a question of length, since in a short novel everything has to be worked in as best it can: Barsad will inevitably turn out to be Miss Pross's long-lost brother, Defarge has to double as Doctor Manette's old servant, and so forth. But there is a deeper reason for feeling more dissatisfaction with the artificial plot here than one does with equally far-fetched situations elsewhere in Dickens. Where society is felt as an all-enveloping force, Dickens is able to turn the melodramatic conventions which he inherited to good use; however preposterous the individual coincidences, they serve an important symbolic function. The world is more of a piece than we suppose, Dickens is saying, and our fates are bound up, however cut off from one another we may appear: the pestilence from Tom-All-Alone's really will spread to the Dedlock mansion, and sooner or later the river in which Gaffer Hexam fishes for corpses will flow through the veneering drawing-room. In a word, we can't have Miss Havisham without Magwitch. But without a thick social atmosphere swirling round them, the characters of *A Tale of Two Cities* stand out in stark melodramatic isolation; the spotlight is trained too sharply on the implausibilities of the plot....

Yet despite the dark mood in which it was conceived, the *Tale* isn't a wholly gloomy work; nor is the final impression which it leaves with us one of a wallow of self-pity on the scaffold. We are told of Darnay in the condemned cell (or is it Carton?) that

> his hold on life was strong, and it was very, very hard to loosen; by gradual efforts and degrees unclosed a little here, it clenched the tighter there; and when he brought his strength to bear on that hand and it yielded, this was closed again. There was a hurry, too, in all his thoughts, a turbulent and heated working of his heart, that contended against resignation. (bk. III, ch. 13)

And near the end, as Miss Pross grapples with Madame Defarge, Dickens speaks of 'the vigorous tenacity of love, always so much stronger than hate'. The gruesome events of the book scarcely bear out such a judgment, yet as an article of faith, if not as a statement of the literal truth, it is curiously impressive. For all the sense of horror which he must have felt stirring within him when he wrote *A Tale of Two Cities*, Dickens remained a moralist and a preacher, and it was his saving strength. But if the author doesn't succumb with Carton, neither does he escape with Darnay.... Nothing is concluded, and by turning his malaise into a work of art Dickens obtains parole, not release: the prison will soon be summoning him once more.

# Stylistic Devices in *A Tale of Two Cities*

Sylvère Monod

Sylvère Monod argues that, despite deficiencies in
*A Tale of Two Cities*, Dickens has deliberately crafted
a masterful style in this novel. Monod explains and
cites examples of four of Dickens's techniques: repetition, cumulative effect, images and comparisons,
and "Revolutionary style." Sylvère Monod is professor of English at the *Institut d'Études Anglaises* of the
Sorbonne in Paris. He has written numerous articles
for scholarly journals and is the author of *Dickens
Romancier*, which has been translated into English.

However intensely one may dislike many aspects of *A Tale of
Two Cities,* however devoutly one would like to discuss its
profounder significance, it must be recognized that the book
possesses, first of all, the quality of superb and masterly
writing. . . . The artistry, or at any rate the craftsmanship,
that went into the writing was entirely deliberate, and it conditions much of the effect, and nearly all the value, the novel
achieves. Under almost every other count—ideas, history,
characters, humor—*A Tale of Two Cities* has repeatedly and
justifiably been found deficient. . . .

A great many of the stylistic characteristics of *A Tale of
Two Cities* have their source in Dickens himself, whose own
influence on his writing is to be felt in two ways. From the
old or usual Dickens derive a number of devices, proce-
dures, and mannerisms adopted, it would seem, because he
could not do otherwise, because he was doomed to be forever, irrepressibly, himself. The new Dickens is the conscious artist, out to write an entirely new kind of book. . . .

Among the new devices most deliberately used by Dickens in *A Tale of Two Cities* repetition clearly holds pride of
place. . . . Typical examples of repetitive processes are only

Excerpted from Sylvère Monod, "Some Stylistic Devices in *A Tale of Two Cities*," in
*Dickens the Craftsman: Strategies of Presentation*, edited, with a foreword by Robert B.
Partlow Jr. (Carbondale: Southern Illinois University Press, 1970). Copyright ©1970 by
Southern Illinois University Press. Reprinted by permission of the publisher.

too easy to encounter in the *Tale*. Almost at random, we come across "Hunger"—with the emphatic capital initial—repeated eight times in fifteen lines (I, *v*); "put to Death" nine times in eleven lines (II, *i*); "poor" ten times (plus "spare" once) within nine lines, followed by "tax" five times in two lines (II, *viii*); "stone" eight times (plus one "stony") in five lines (II, *ix*). Repetition can be used on a smaller scale, but also, characteristically, in "the gloomy tile-paved entry to the gloomy tile-paved staircase" (I, *v*), or "his heart grew heavier again, and grew yet heavier and heavier every day . . . with a heart growing heavier and heavier" (II, *xviii*).

In the above examples repetition is concentrated over a small number of lines. In other cases, words and phrases are repeated many times in a more spread-out way; they are not likely to have escaped the attention of any reader of the *Tale*, yet it may be suggestive to bring some of them together. Stryver's "shouldering" and "delicacy," contrasted with Carton's "carelessness" and "no delicacy," and the "lion and jackal" contrast are tirelessly iterated by Dickens and emphasized by several chapter headings. . . .

"Knitting" is another famous term in the novel: it suggests one or two observations. On the one hand, since Madame Defarge is forever knitting from the very beginning of her novelistic career (I, *vi*, where she knits sitting, standing, and even walking) and infects her friend with the habit, it is something of a mystery in such a poor country, where bread is so scarce and where wool has to come from the same source as even scarcer mutton: no knitted article of clothing is ever produced; knitting is a luxury, and it is thus in one sense gratuitous but in another, inevitably, expensive. Secondly, Dickens achieves through sheer repetition the remarkable result of turning the very word "knitting" from the name of a useful or at worst innocent pastime into something sinister, ominous, and even murderous: when we see Madame Defarge "pointing her knitting-needle at Little Lucie as if it were the finger of Fate" (III, *iii*), we realize that it is more like a sword or a dagger than anything else. And when Defarge is shown "speaking with knitted brows" (III, *i*), we protest that it is an awkward mistake, for his house is one in which, not brows, but Dooms, are being knitted. . . .

The "theme with variations" procedure . . . is related to another noteworthy device which may be called the cumulative effect, an effect obtained by the accumulation of many words connected with one main idea. A study of the vocabulary used by Dickens in any random paragraph of *A Tale of Two Cities* is nearly always suggestive from that point of view. Some sections might serve (and have in fact been so employed) as lessons in English vocabulary. When Dr. Manette's recovered energy is described (II, *vi*), within some ten lines are to be found, not only the words "energy" (twice) and "energetic," but also the phrases "great firmness of purpose . . . strength of resolution . . . vigour of action"; and the reader is further told that the Doctor "sustained a great deal of fatigue with ease." This profusion of words, all of which are accurately distinguished, produces an impression of masterly and inexhaustible resourcefulness. Mr. Lorry's prospective visions of his impending encounter with Manette provide remarkable examples: "They differed principally in . . . the ghastliness of their worn and wasted state. Pride, contempt, defiance, stubbornness, submission, lamentation, succeeded one another; so did varieties of sunken cheek, cadaverous colour, emaciated hands and figures" (I, *iii*). The Defarges' staircase is not a pleasant place; its brilliant description contains the following words: "vile . . . foul . . . heaps of refuse . . . other refuse . . . uncontrollable and hopeless mass of decomposition . . . polluted the air . . . intangible impurities . . . bad sources . . . insupportable . . . a dark shaft of dirt and poison . . . corrupted . . . spoilt and sickly vapours" (I, *v*).

These examples show the nature of the device. But, like repetition, cumulative effects can be made to serve several distinct purposes. One of the most interesting is its use for conveying psychological observations. If the novelist's purpose is to show that Carton is careless, he will show him "leaning back, with his gown torn half off him, his untidy wig, . . . his eyes on the ceiling, . . . something especially reckless in his demeanour," and later, once more "careless . . . lounging . . . loitering" (II, *iii*). . . .

In other cases, the cumulative process is clearly used for the creation of atmosphere. The quietness of the Soho corner (II, *vi*) is suggested by "quiet . . . quaint . . . retirement . . . cool spot, staid but cheerful . . . a very harbour . . . a tranquil bark . . . little was audible . . . shunned by all . . . a lonely lodger." The gradual trapping and imprisonment of Darnay in France (III, *i*) is emphasized by the constant hammering of many words: "barrier . . . closed and strongly guarded . . .

prisoner . . . escort . . . prisoner . . . escort and escorted . . .
guard-room . . . gate . . . the gate was held by a mixed
guard . . . ingress was easy enough, egress was very difficult . . . barrier . . . guard . . . barrier . . . escort . . . escorted
. . . guard-room . . . guardhouse.". . .

## IMAGES AND COMPARISONS

Images and comparisons of all kinds, from the ordinary sim-
ile up to the most elaborate metaphors and symbols, form
the third major stylistic device in the *Tale.* . . .

In the first place, the persistence of some traditionally
Dickensian methods is clearly to be observed. Images prolif-
erate in the *Tale* as elsewhere; even the stupidest characters,
like the road-mender, are credited with some imaginative
and metaphorical powers: "Some whisper this, some whisper that; they speak of nothing else; even the fountain appears to fall to that tune" (II, *xv*). The usual anthropomorphic[1] treatment of inanimate objects (mainly houses, doors,
and pieces of furniture) reappears again and again: "a loud
watch, ticking a sonorous sermon" (I, *iv*); "a door of idiotic
obstinacy with a weak rattle in its throat" (II, *i*); another
door "grudgingly turned on its hinges" (II, *ii*). Of this procedure there exist variants: instead of anthropomorphic an
image can be zoomorphic[2] ("the little . . . town of Dover hid
itself away from the beach, and ran its head into the chalk
cliffs, like a marine ostrich" in I, *iv*) or theomorphic[3] (as in
the legend of the guillotine in III, *iv*). The anthropomorphic
device is occasionally used in reverse, when a human being
is treated as an inanimate object: Jerry throws off "sarcastic
sparks from the whirling grindstone of his indignation"
(II, *i*) and behaves like "an animated bit of the spiked wall of
Newgate" (II, *ii*). Parts of the body can also be detached for
similar purpose: "Mr. Lorry shook his head; using that important part of himself as a sort of fairy cloak that would fit
anything" (II, *vi*). In addition to the successful images of this
specific type, there are others which are pleasantly characteristic of Dickens' usual manner through their picturesque-
ness or their poetry: Jerry wears "an old cocked-hat like a
three-cornered spittoon" (I, *iii*). . . .

Secondly, some images are used in specific ways to serve

---

1. attributing human qualities to nonhuman objects and animals   2. attributing animal qualities to nonanimal objects   3. depicting humans or objects as having the
qualities of a god

the special purposes of the *Tale*. There is a kind of symboli-
cal color-scheme: red is the color of blood, of wine, and the
setting sun. The point is, if not labored, certainly emphasized: "The sunset struck so brilliantly into the travelling
carriage ... that its occupant was steeped in crimson"
(II, *viii*); "in the glow, the water of the chateau seemed to
turn to blood, and the stone faces crimsoned" (II, *ix*); the
French road-mender himself says that he saw some soldiers,
and adds, "They were almost black to my sight—except on
the side of the sun going to bed, where they have a red edge,
messieurs" (II, *vx*). . . .

## REVOLUTIONARY STYLE

The term "Revolutionary style" which I use to label the
fourth category of specific stylistic devices in the *Tale* may
not be the most adequate phrase, but it is a tempting one.
Dickens is increasingly recognized as a revolutionary writer
(in his treatment of language), although this went almost
unperceived by most of his contemporaries and was re-
sented by the rest. When he deals with the French Revolution, his theme, it seems to me, reinforces a tendency that
was already in existence. At the core of this phenomenon is
to be observed the interplay between rhetoric (which implies order and control) and exaltation (which involves irre-
pressible outbursts).

Dickens' mastery over his medium had never been so
complete. His longest sentences remain clear; his handling
of intricate syntax is skillful; his control is perfect whenever
he wishes to exert it. . . .

The plentiful use of rhetoric—a code of rules ensuring or-
derliness so as to achieve effectiveness and persuasiveness—
strengthens Dickens' superb control over his writing. In a
book with a historical, philosophical, and political message,
the author wants and needs to persuade the reader. Some of
the devices already studied are rhetorical: repetition, symmetry, and imagery are parts of rhetoric. But there are other
arts of persuasion whose use in the *Tale* must be described.
They are probably what G.K. Chesterton had in mind when
he wrote of the *Tale* that "in dignity and eloquence it almost
stands alone among his books." The composition of many
paragraphs, the marshaling of the words in them, is eloquent;
they are made for effect and they achieve it. The end, that is,
the last three paragraphs of II, *v*, is a clear illustration, though

too long for quotation. A briefer and proportionately neater example is to be found in II, *xiii:* "When Mr. Stryver . . . had carried his delicacy into Devonshire, and when the sight and scent of flowers in the City streets had some waifs of goodness in them for the worst, of health for the sickliest, and of youth for the oldest, Sydney's feet still trod those stones.". . .

---

### THE ELOQUENCE OF DICKENS'S RHETORICAL STYLE

*In the following excerpt, Dickens crafts sentences with repetition, imagery, and symmetry, effectively using a description of a morning walk on the street to convey Carton's sense of failure.*

When his host followed him out on the staircase with a candle, to light him down the stairs, the day was coldly looking in through its grimy windows. When he got out of the house, the air was cold and sad, the dull sky overcast, the river dark and dim, the whole scene like a lifeless desert. And wreaths of dust were spinning round and round before the morning blast, as if the desert-sand had risen far away, and the first spray of it in its advance had begun to overwhelm the city.

Waste forces within him, and a desert all around, this man stood still on his way across a silent terrace, and saw for a moment, lying in the wilderness before him, a mirage of honourable ambition, self-denial, and perseverance. In the fair city of this vision, there were airy galleries from which the loves and graces looked upon him, gardens in which the fruits of life hung ripening, waters of Hope that sparkled in his sight. A moment, and it was gone. Climbing to a high chamber in a well of houses, he threw himself down in his clothes on a neglected bed, and its pillow was wet with wasted tears.

Sadly, sadly, the sun rose; it rose upon no sadder sight than the man of good abilities and good emotions, incapable of their directed exercise, incapable of his own help and his own happiness, sensible of the blight on him, and resigning himself to let it eat him away.

---

Dickens' idea in such cases seems to be that intense purposefulness and single-mindedness tend, especially in a Frenchman, to produce or reinforce rhetorical inclinations. And that is true enough. The final sentence of the book, spoken, not by a Frenchman, but by a character with a French-sounding name, one who had studied in Paris, is a perfect specimen of rhetorical symmetry: "It is a far, far better thing that I do, than I have ever done; it is a far, far better rest that I go to, than I have ever known."

Yet, under the influence of the vivid and contradictory emotions created in him by the violence of the revolutionary episodes, Dickens seems to lose his fine control. He becomes overexcited; his style is disrupted; his sentences explode. It may be deliberate policy on his part thus to let himself go or even to work himself up into a state of frenzy. The result, at any rate, is striking. . . .

One of the earliest sentences referring to the revolutionary happenings is remarkable by its lush "verbfulness"; it concerns Defarge who, within three lines, "issued orders, issued arms, thrust this man back, dragged this man forward, disarmed one man to arm another, laboured and strove." Such is the initial impulse; once it had been given, the Revolution is set going and acquires its own momentum. Hence the new and more properly revolutionary style, in which the most violent actions are described in conspicuously verbless sentences, through the juxtaposition of brief separate vignettes, like the storming of the Bastille: "Deep ditches, double drawbridge, massive stone walls, eight great towers, cannon, muskets, fire and smoke." It is as though Dickens had invented a kind of cinematographic technique: each image is motionless, but their quick succession produces an impression of motion. . . .

When the revolutionary disruption is combined with other devices (rhetoric, imagery, cumulative vocabulary, and repetition), a few genuine prose poems can be the result of their association. The end of II, *ix*, relating the death of the Marquis, and Carton's night walk through the streets of Paris (III, *ix*) are remarkable pieces of elaborate and, on the whole, felicitous writing. As for Carton's death itself (III, *xv*), if one concentrates on the wording without reacting to the complex of emotions involved, it may be regarded as a miniature masterpiece in that kind. After a final repetition of the Gospel phrase about the "Resurrection and the Life," it consists merely in this: "The murmuring of many voices, the upturning of many faces, the pressing on of many footsteps in the outskirts of the crowd, so that it swells forward in a mass, like one great heave of water, all flashes away. Twenty-three.". . .

Few would refuse to admit that the *Tale* is very much a contrived product. It should, however, in all fairness, be stated that the contrivance is less obvious in passages of dialogue or ordinary description of things and gestures than in narrative and comment; that the contrivance is usually superb; that it is entirely intentional, part of the author's deliberate attempt at stylization and connected with the authoritative tone he usually adopted after *David Copperfield.* If one objection to the *Tale,* proffered by people who like Dickens better in his relaxed Pickwickian mood, is that it is a tense book, it may be confessed that it is so.

# Fantasy and Reality in *Great Expectations*

Paul Pickrel

Paul Pickrel argues that Dickens reveals his moral view through contrasting characters and plot. Pickrel shows how Dickens uses the plot to portray his view of moral reality, which acknowledges both the dark and the light, the disappointments and the hopes of human experience. Paul Pickrel has taught English at Smith College. He has published reviews of numerous books in journals and is the author of a novel, *The Moving Stairs*.

*Great Expectations* is in the first place a fantasy. It is a fantasy of a sort that many children have; perhaps all children have it, and certainly all lonely children, all children who feel too little wanted or appreciated, who feel the powerlessness of childhood. Nor is it a fantasy limited to children; anyone who buys a chance on a Cadillac or a sweepstakes ticket shares it, and probably it plays a larger part in the fantasy life of adults than most of us would care to admit. It is a fantasy of sudden translation or sudden transformation, the fantasy of arrival at a point where yearning is magically fulfilled, commonly expressed in such phrases as "when I get rich" or "when my ship comes in." It is a fantasy of a beneficent if unpredictable universe that will someday shower us with gold without any effort or indeed any merit on our part.

Pip, the main character and the narrator in *Great Expectations*, is a little boy at the beginning of the novel. He is an orphan who has been "brought up by hand" by his much older sister, the harsh and loveless Mrs. Joe Gargery. In the normal course of events he will be apprenticed to his brother-in-law, the blacksmith of Joe Gargery; he will learn blacksmithing, and he will live out his days working beside Joe at the forge, perhaps someday marrying Biddy, an un-

Excerpted from Paul Pickrel, "Teaching the Novel: *Great Expectations*," in *Essays in the Teaching of English*, edited by Edward J. Gordon and Edward S. Noyes (New York: Appleton-Century-Crofts, 1960). Copyright ©1960 by National Council of Teachers of English. Reprinted courtesy of the NCTE.

kempt little girl who helps her old grandmother run a miserable evening school for the children of the village.

## FANTASTIC CHARACTERS IN PIP'S LIFE

But two powerful, fantastic figures come into Pip's life and change its course. One is Magwitch, the criminal. He erupts in the first chapter, when Pip is out in a graveyard on the marshes one cold Christmas Eve. Magwitch is a convict escaped from the prison ship, the Hulks, "the wicked Noah's ark." He is in leg irons, cold, hungry, desperate. He is everything that a weak and passive child fears in the adult world: its capacity for wickedness, the brutality of its emotions, its strength and violence and consummate egoism, the threat of being utterly outcast and utterly alone. Magwitch demands that Pip steal food for him from Mrs. Joe Gargery's larder and a file for his leg irons from Joe's forge, and in terror of his life Pip does both. That is apparently the end of the incident, but the first encounter with the convict on the marshes that cold winter twilight leaves a slimy trail across Pip's life—a trail of prisons and criminals and crime—until years later when Magwitch erupts again.

The other fantastic figure in Pip's world is Miss Havisham, a rich old woman who represents the promise of adulthood as much as Magwitch represents its threat. At first glance, this is an extraordinary role for her to play, for her whole life has been sacrificed to memorializing the frustration of her own hopes, in commemorating the moment when the man who was supposed to marry her failed to show up for the wedding. Her clocks stand stopped at that hour, she has never since seen the light of day, she sits in her ruined wedding dress, one ruined white satin slipper still in her hand, the ruined wedding feast spread in the room across the hall, the only guests coming unbidden from behind the plaster. The very name of her once fine house is a mockery: it is "Satis House"—"enough house"—so called in boast by the ancestor who built it because he vainly supposed that whoever had such a house could never want for more, although Miss Havisham, the last of her family, has lived out her years there in testimony to the corrosion of all great expectations, whether based upon the love of man or the seeming certitude of stone.

The reason Miss Havisham can represent the promise of adulthood, in spite of her own ruin, comes partly from the fact that she is rich and partly because she is not alone. She has an adopted daughter, Estella, a little girl as beautiful and coldly distant as the star whose name she bears. Like many people who have made one great self-denying gesture, Miss Havisham is abandonedly self-indulgent, giving a free reign to her whims and self-pity. Adopting Estella was an act of indulgence on her part: bored and foolish, she keeps the child as a plaything, and rears her on a principle of vengeance, carefully cultivating Estella's beauty so that she can grow up to break the hearts of men.

Out of her impatience to see what effect Estella will have on a representative of the male sex, Miss Havisham sends down word that she wants a little boy to come and play in her rooms, and the boy who lives at the blacksmith's, Pip, is the one hit upon. When he appears at Satis House Miss Havisham has reason to congratulate herself: Pip is hopelessly smitten by Estella's beauty; in the presence of her superior manners he realizes the crudity of his own upbringing and the vast difference that stretches between Joe Gargery's forge and the polite world. He and Estella play a card game called "Beggar Your Neighbor," and while Miss Havisham croaks out in the background, "Beggar him, beggar him," Estella proceeds to do just that.

Pip dares not speak of Magwitch to anyone, and he cannot tell the truth about what happens at Miss Havisham's. When pressed for details he lies outrageously: Miss Havisham and Estella belong too much to the world of fantasy to be shared with his companions in everyday reality. In their dark, candlelit rooms, they are fairy godmother and the beautiful princess of a fairy tale, and the thick-fingered, badly dressed, ill-mannered boy from the forge must defend them against any suggestion that they might belong to the daylight world.

A few years pass. Pip is apprentice to Joe Gargery, and Miss Havisham pays his premium as an apprentice, in this way rewarding him for past services, and indicating that his relationship with Satis House is at an end. He was good enough for Estella to practice heartbreak on when she was a child, but now Estella is being trained for bigger game.

Cut off from the figures who have nourished his fantasy, no longer content with the humble expectations Joe Gargery had foreseen for his 'prentice days—those larks they were going to have together—Pip sees in the very landscape of the village a token of his lost hopes: he sees himself like the lowly marshes, while Estella is more distant than ever.

## PIP'S OPPORTUNITY FOR EXPECTATIONS

Then comes the most fantastic stroke of all. Suddenly from London the lawyer, Mr. Jaggers, appears at Joe's with the information that Pip has expectations—great expectations—after all. An anonymous benefactor has decided to lavish luxury and education on the boy, to turn him into a "gentleman." The translation that will put Pip on an equal footing with Estella is to take place; the shower of gold begins to fall. Someone—can it be anyone other than the fairy godmother?—has waved a wand; surely the boy from the forge is destined for the glittering princess.

The story is, then, a fairy tale, with a terrible ogre, Magwitch, a wildly eccentric fairy godmother, an exquisite princess, and a sudden magical transformation. But it is not only a fairy tale, for it is set in a moral universe. One beauty of the life of fantasy, and one reason some of us devote so much time to it, is that it is free from considerations of good and evil. In fantasy we kill off our friends and relatives with impunity; we grow rich without effort; we bestow lavish presents without impoverishing ourselves; we live in immense houses without concern for the servant problem. The moral universe is quite different from that: there our acts have consequences, our choices matter, our privileges entail responsibilities.

## REALISTIC CHARACTERS IN PIP'S LIFE

Now, just as Dickens defines the world of fantasy by two characters, or groups of characters, Magwitch on the one hand, and Miss Havisham and Estella on the other, so he defines the moral universe by two groups of characters, one group centered on Pip's brother-in-law, the blacksmith Joe Gargery, and the other centered on the London lawyer, Mr. Jaggers, who brings Pip word of his great expectations. Or perhaps that is not quite accurate: Dickens uses Joe and Mr. Jaggers not to define the moral universe—that is done by the plot—but rather to personify or embody two different attitudes toward it.

Joe lives by truth to feeling and Mr. Jaggers lives by truth to fact. Joe characteristically looks at a situation as a whole and relates himself to it as his heart bids him. Mr. Jaggers characteristically breaks the situation down into "evidence" and disposes of the evidence in whatever way his mind tells him is appropriate. Joe holds a poetic or symbolic view of experience; Mr. Jaggers holds an analytical [one]. . . .

At the bottom the difference between the two men lies in a difference in their sense of how things are related in the universe and, consequently, in their sense of how an individual can relate himself to them. This comes out most strikingly when we look at the way the two men have behaved in roughly parallel situations. Before the novel opens each man has come across a mother and baby, and each man has responded to the situation in a highly characteristic manner. Joe Gargery came across Pip and his older sister, who was attempting to bring the baby up singlehanded. Joe wanted to help the child, and he did so by embracing the situation as a whole. Though the sister was a termagant with little in her nature to bring the idea of matrimony to a man's mind, Joe married her and so became a kind of father to the baby. Mr. Jaggers, on the other hand, came across a young woman with a baby girl, and his method of dealing with the situation was to separate them. The child he put out for adoption where she would never know who her mother was, and the mother he took into his own house, not on terms of affection but as a servant kept in place by terror. The situations are not strictly parallel, because the future Mrs. Joe Gargery was only a shrew, whereas Mr. Jaggers' future servant was actually a criminal and her baby daughter the child of another criminal, but there is enough similarity to indicate the moral points of view of the two men.

Another way that the difference is dramatized is in the way the two men relate themselves to Pip. Joe's relationship is based upon feeling for the boy, and he allows nothing to cloud the purity of that feeling. . . . Mr. Jaggers, on the other hand, never tires of telling Pip that in their relationship he is acting purely as a businessman. Mr. Jaggers does not approve of the unknown benefactor's scheme and says so; he has no confidence that Pip will profit by his expectations and says so; he is simply carrying out instructions. . . .

There are several curious things Dickens does with the characters of Joe and Mr. Jaggers. For one thing, they are both men, and for another they are both good men. More recent English novelists who have tried to defend the poetic view of experience ordinarily use a woman to embody it, and ordinarily make her superior to those who represent another view. . . . But Dickens uses men to embody both the poetic and the analytic view of experience. . . .

Often it seems that what I have called the poetic view of life—the feeling that things somehow hang together and make sense, that we can somehow relate ourselves as a whole to experience—often it seems that the only argument in favor of that view of life is our profound need of it. But Dickens saw a stronger argument, and in *Great Expectations* he advances it as a novelist ought to advance his arguments —by the plot.

## THE PLOT DEFINES DICKENS' POINT OF VIEW

The plot of *Great Expectations is* a good one; it holds the reader's interest; it is full of surprises and odd turns; its complexities all come out neatly in the end. But more than that, it is a symbolic representation of Dickens' vision of the moral universe, and the chief characteristic of that vision is that good and evil, what we most desire and what we most loathe, are inextricably intertwined, involved with one another in such a way that no human hand can sort them out.

The plot is resolved through the discovery of a series of surprising relationships, and each of these is a relationship between something loathsome and something desirable. The first of these is the discovery that Pip does not owe his great expectations to the fairy godmother, Miss Havisham, but to the ogre, Magwitch. Magwitch has been transported to Australia; there he has prospered as a sheep rancher, and he has decided to use his wealth to make a gentleman of the little boy who stole the food and file for him on the marshes long ago. Pip's rise in the world has not been an act of magic; it has actually been a reward for theft, for what he has regarded as the most shameful deed of his life.

The second great discovery is that Estella, whom Pip has wasted his life in loving, is far from being a princess; she is in fact the illegitimate daughter of Magwitch by the criminal who now serves as Mr. Jaggers' servant. Miss Havisham is no fairy godmother; she is a foolish old meddler.

Life is not, Dickens is showing us symbolically by the plot, a dungheap in which one can find an occasional jewel to pluck out, as Mr. Jaggers supposes. It is an old, old growth; the fairest flower and the most noxious weed have their roots in the same ancient soil. Joe Gargery's view of experience is right because he has grasped this fact—not intellectually, for Joe is no intellectual, but by accepting in love the complexity of the moral universe. In Lear's phrase, he has taken upon himself the mystery of things.

Pip himself represents an impure mixture of the easiest parts of both Joe's and Mr. Jaggers' attitudes toward experience.

Actually it is not altogether fair to compare Pip with Joe and Mr. Jaggers: they are unchanging, fixed points of reference in the book—so much so that they seem never to age. But Pip changes. When first we meet him he is an innocent little boy. When last we see him he is a man in early middle age, much chastened by experience. The book is essentially an account of Pip's moral education. . . .

Pip differs from both men. He is not a realist; he is a fantasist. He supposes that he can have the best of both views and the unfavorable consequences of neither. He embraces isolation, as Mr. Jaggers does, but he embraces it selectively—or, in other words, he becomes a terrible snob. He cuts himself off from his own past—he neglects Joe, he does not go back to the forge, he is ashamed of his blacksmith's arm among the languid or vicious young bloods whose society he cultivates in London. He isolates himself from those who love him, but he does not accept the natural consequence of his action, which is lovelessness. Love is as necessary to Pip as to Joe Gargery, but Pip wants it on his own terms, the terms of fantasy. He can only love the fairy-tale princess, the coldly glittering distant star, Estella.

Now Pip is not entirely to be blamed in all this. His early life *was* fantastic; his contacts with creatures like Magwitch and Miss Havisham could only encourage the habit of fantasy in him; and then in adolescence to have his wildest dreams realized, to be suddenly transformed from a humble village apprentice to a young Londoner with great expectations— what result could all this have except to make the boy suppose that the world is indeed whatever his fancy would like it to be? How could he avoid supposing that he was one singularly excused by the gods from facing consequences? . . .

The novel ends with Pip and Estella reunited at the gate of the ruined Satis House. As you probably know, Dickens originally had them simply meet and part, presumably forever; but his friend Bulwer Lytton prevailed upon him to supply the "happier" ending. Some readers have deplored the alteration; to me it seems not to matter, for by this point Estella has been so thoroughly discredited as a creature of fantasy and Pip so thoroughly discredited as a fantasist that they are hardly the same people they once were; they are at most a middle-aged couple who have failed.

The healing touch at the end of the novel is not the reunion of Pip and Estella, but Pip's return to the forge. By the time he goes back, his sister, Mrs. Joe Gargery, has long since died, and the ageless Joe has married Biddy, the girl whom Pip might once have married had he been free of the myth of his own life. They have a child, a little boy, and they have named him Pip. "And there was I again!" the old Pip cries to himself. Another generation has come along; another branch of that ancient vine, the human race, has sprung forth. Its roots are in the tangled dark, as ours are; they will have to learn to live with that fact, as we must; but perhaps, acknowledging the dark, they will do a better job of seeking the light.

# Multiple Narratives in *Great Expectations*

Nicola Bradbury

Nicola Bradbury argues that Dickens creates suspense in *Great Expectations* by interweaving several narratives into Pip's story, keeping the reader wondering how the pieces will fit together. Bradbury cites transitional chapters 6 and 7 and chapter 47 to show how Dickens creates suspense even in lulls between Pip's expectations. According to Bradbury, Dickens's multiple stories also enrich the theme of the novel. Nicola Bradbury is the author of *Henry James: The Later Novels* and *An Annotated Critical Bibliography of Henry James* as well as numerous articles on literary criticism published in journals.

Revelation competes with secrecy to control the structure of *Great Expectations.* The novel was first published in weekly parts, each containing just one or two chapters. The next division was in nine monthly numbers. Finally the book came out in three volumes: one for each stage of Pip's expectations. So Dickens turned publishing constrictions into structural resources. He used each unit (from sentence and paragraph to chapter and part, number or volume) to measure out the narrative, not as a flow, but a discrete series of anticipations and disappointments, expectations and recognitions—each one, even the last, vitally incomplete. The age-old, informal contract between story-teller and audience for attention to be rewarded with interest is highly organised. Through this technique Dickens refines the processes of narrative so that they not only give the pleasures of suspense, surprise, or gratified expectation, but act as a structural counterpart to the very experiences Pip is undergoing within the narrative. Furthermore, this effect of replication is amplified within the novel by two means: the

Excerpted from Nicola Bradbury, *Charles Dickens'* Great Expectations. Copyright ©1990 by Nicola Bradbury. Reprinted with permission of St. Martin's Press, Inc.

first person narration, and the inclusion together with Pip's central story of a whole series of subordinate narratives which both feed into and reflect on his: the story of Joe, of Biddy, of Estella, of Herbert, of Miss Havisham, for example, and of course the story of Magwitch.

Narrative technique, narrative structure and the narrative line itself therefore interlock in *Great Expectations* in the treatment of the 'expectation' theme. The title encourages us to look forward; the narrator is looking back: there is a possibility of fantasy, a risk of mere historical report—but between them, the shifting, fascinating processes of exploration, corresponding to imagination, memory and reflection.

We can approach this subtlety step by step. Looking first at the units of composition, then analysing the structural features of the narrative line, and finally considering the counterpoint[1] of single and multiple focus of narratives, we can deconstruct the shape and measure the pacing of the novel.

## UNITS OF COMPOSITION AND THEIR MEANING

Three volumes form the principal structure of *Great Expectations,* distinguishing the stages of longing (Chapters 1 to 19), the 'gay fiction' of enjoyment (Chapters 20 to 39) and disillusionment (Chapters 40 to 59). These phases are punctuated by the two great narrative surprises: the bequest, and the revelation of the benefactor. Ironically, these events, which strike Pip with astonishment, are seen on reflection to form an inseparable pair. They are, moreover, part of a sequence which begins with the very first page of the novel; when Magwitch appears, and continues to the last page when his daughter Estella is brought together with Pip. So the dramatic 'peripeteia' and 'catastrophe' (the sudden turn and subversion of order) do not, after all, interrupt, but they constitute the narrative flow. It is a story moving through anticipation and disappointment to recognition. Self-recognition, indeed, for it is Pip's self-knowledge which depends on his stopping to review his own story and see that it is not what he thought it was, but a different kind, with different principal characters, a different plot and a very different tone. He has to shift his point of view, and 'reread' his life.

Suspense develops from a negative device in this process

---

1. in music the technique of combining two or more melodic lines into a harmonic whole

towards a metaphysical condition: the 'negative capability' which Keats described as a function of genius, 'that is when man is capable of being in uncertainties, Mysteries, doubts, without any irritable reaching after fact & reason' (letter to George and Tom Keats, 21 December 1817). When Pip is promised a fortune, secrecy is imposed upon him against the itch of his curiosity; when the benefactor is revealed, he learns a deeper mystery, and comes to accept it. Dickens conducts us through suspense, which has an end, into wonder, which may be endless: the first is embroiled with worldliness, but the second shifts to a different scale of values. Suspense relies on expectation; but wonder comes, paradoxically, out of disappointment. The movement between them, back and forth, is a constant tension throughout the novel and it operates in every unit of the structure, from the whole, or the volume, to the individual chapter, paragraph, or sentence. Pip's stance, and ours, is never securely fixed.

## THE FUNCTION OF TRANSITIONAL CHAPTERS 6 AND 7

Dickens's control, however, is secure. He not only sustains excitement through significant incidents, but with remarkable economy he makes good use of the intervening passages: pages which might seem unimportant. A fine example comes in Chapters 6 and 7: the two chapters which formed the fourth weekly part of the novel when it was first published and concluded the first 'number' in the monthly issue. These chapters have the tricky function of easing the novel from the vital first incident with Magwitch on the marshes into the 'second subject', when Pip is summoned to Satis House. How is Dickens to make this transition, without losing the interest of the audience, and yet avoid violating the secret parallel between the 'two openings', and between Magwitch and Miss Havisham, on which Pip's misconception, and the whole course of the novel, is to depend?

The answer is distance, of tone and subject matter, disguising thematic relevance. The transitional passage, a single publishing unit, is divided into two chapters. The first (6) is short, retrospective, rather serious. The second (7) is lengthy, wandering, often comical. Both seem to pause, relax from the concentration of 'great expectations'. The narrative scarcely advances, the pressure is released. Yet in this lull that aspect of Pip's story which has less to do with his fortunes than his personal development has space to grow. The issues of moral cowardice and responsibility are conjoined in Chapter 6 when Pip wonders whether to tell Joe his guilty secret. He decides not to, for fear of losing Joe's confidence. This concealment is, of course, a precondition of the novel's story. But the preternaturally adult language in which it is recorded, the abstraction and ethical weighting, act as clues to the importance of this decision on a thematic level, distinct from the plot. If we pick up these clues, then even the apparent simplicity of the last sentence in this chapter begins to seem disingenuous. We hear a warning. These matters are not to be forgotten even if the story turns away from them for a while: 'My state of mind, as I have described it, began before I was up in the morning, and lasted long after the subject had died out, and had ceased to be mentioned saving on exceptional occasions'.

Pip's confession is one of a long series of clues, narrative and stylistic, that—together with his story as it appeared to the characters surrounding him, or even to Pip himself at the time—another, hidden text is unfolding: the ironic, comical, pathetic and significant narrative which is available now to the grown man, and which may become open to us, if we read with full awareness.

This 'subtext' is what provides the rationale for Chapter 7. What looks on the surface like slack composition, wandering from Pip's early lesson to the story of Joe's childhood and then back to Pip and the summons to Satis House, works obliquely towards demonstrating the central development of the novel. The Satis House adventure at the end of the chapter will be a learning experience, just as much as Pip's first letters which begin it. Between them, Joe's history of childhood neglect, quarrelling parents, violence and tyrannical possessiveness, with his patient, loving and selfless response, does more than explain his character and Pip's background, or Mrs Joe's situation. It also stands for comparison with Magwitch's history, and Estella's, Miss Havisham's, Pip's own. So we are nudged towards a process of interpretation in the course of the chapter, when the young Pip, consoling Joe for Mrs Joe's grim appearance, 'sagaciously observed, if it didn't signify to him, to whom did it signify?' In fact, all appearances in this world are significant—if not always in the way they first seem—and all significance is general: it is a system of expression which

unites people in understanding, and divides them only
when it is misconceived. The importance of Joe's example is
recognised in Chapter 7, though it is so soon to be forgotten,
and only much later fully appreciated. Pip as a child

> dated a new admiration of Joe from that night. We were
> equals afterwards, as we had been before; but afterwards at
> quiet times when I sat looking at Joe and thinking about him,
> I had a new sensation of feeling conscious that I was looking
> up to Joe in my heart.

## THE PACE AND MELODRAMA OF CHAPTER 47

A different example of structural pacing comes in Chapter
47. The opening of the eighth monthly number, at the middle of volume three, is not apparently an important position.
Pip is here marking time, waiting for the moment to escape
with Magwitch. He has lost all hope of Estella: 'an impression settled heavily on me that she was married', though he
avoids discovering whether this is true. Pip's despondency
fits both this emotional impasse and the enforced inactivity
with Magwitch. It is appropriate to the suspended plot; but
such gloom inevitably jeopardises the narrative excitement
which an author-in-series can never afford to abandon. How
does Dickens satisfy these contradictory requirements: to
have the novel slow to a pause, and yet urge the reader on?

The chapter begins with Pip's helpless mood, the emotional counterpart to suspended action. To vary the monotony, Pip decides to go to the play before returning to bed.
What he sees is a musical comedy followed by 'the last new
grand Christmas pantomime': a spectacle calculated to introduce variety. It is an opportunity Dickens willingly ex-
ploits for a ludicrous interlude. The hapless Wopsle has
sunk from Hamlet to this! His former pretensions are not
without significance, however, for just as once the black-
stockinged figure encountered his 'royal phantom', so now
'Mr Wopsle with red worsted legs under a highly magnified
phosphoric countenance and a shock of red curtain-fringe
for his hair' sees a ghost. This revenant is not on stage, however, but in the audience, sitting immediately behind the
unconscious Pip. It is the very incarnation of Pip's secret
anxieties, both about the past and the haunted present: Magwitch's enemy, Compeyson.

This incident is the height of melodrama, the furthest
stretch of coincidence, yet in the telling, Dickens stresses,

rather than conceals, these outrages to probability. As with the first appearance of Magwitch, or the first glimpse of Compeyson himself, it is this quality of assault which is most vital—for it is this which violates the safe discrimination of dreams or nightmares from waking reality, and intrudes the most fearful threat: one which half seems to come from inside.

Pip's response is not hysterical. On the contrary, his con-

### PIP'S STRUGGLE WITH HIS CONSCIENCE

*In the transitional chapter 6, Pip considers telling Joe his secret concerning the convict, but recoils from the disclosure in fear of losing his companionship with Joe.*

My state of mind regarding the pilfering from which I had been so unexpectedly exonerated, did not impel me to frank disclosure; but I hope it had some dregs of good at the bottom of it.

I do not recall that I felt any tenderness of conscience in reference to Mrs. Joe, when the fear of being found out was lifted off me. But I loved Joe—perhaps for no better reason in those early days than because the dear fellow let me love him—and, as to him, my inner self was not so easily composed. It was much upon my mind (particularly when I first saw him looking about for his file) that I ought to tell Joe the whole truth. Yet I did not, and for the reason that I mistrusted that if I did, he would think me worse than I was. The fear of losing Joe's confidence, and of thenceforth sitting in the chimney corner at night staring drearily at my for ever lost companion and friend, tied up my tongue. I morbidly represented to myself that if Joe knew it, I never afterwards could see him at the fireside feeling his fair whisker, without thinking that he was meditating on it. That, if Joe knew it, I never afterwards could see him glance, however casually, at yesterday's meat or pudding when it came on to-day's table, without thinking that he was debating whether I had been in the pantry. That, if Joe knew it, and at any subsequent period of our joint domestic life remarked that his beer was flat or thick, the conviction that he suspected Tar in it, would bring a rush of blood to my face. In a word, I was too cowardly to do what I knew to be right, as I had been too cowardly to avoid doing what I knew to be wrong. I had had no intercourse with the world at that time, and I imitated none of its many inhabitants who act in this manner. Quite an untaught genius, I made the discovery of the line of action for myself.

trolled disquiet, mirrored in complex and balanced sentence rhythms circling around repeated words and phrases, opposes reason against horror:

> I cannot exaggerate the enhanced disquiet into which this conversation threw me, or the special and peculiar terror I felt at Compeyson's having been behind me 'like a ghost'. For, if he had even been out of my thoughts for a few moments together since the hiding had begun, it was in those very moments when he was closest to me; and to think that I should be so unconscious and off my guard after all my care, was as if I had shut an avenue of a hundred doors to keep him out, and then had found him at my elbow. I could not doubt either that he was there, because I was there, and that however slight an appearance of danger there might be about us, danger was always near and active.

There is a fine ambiguity in 'I could not doubt . . . that he was there, because I was there' ('I could not doubt . . . because', or, 'he was there, because'): doubt and certainty turn on the differing logic of the conscious and subconscious mind, laying bare the lines of the story. The contamination of Pip's calculation by nagging fear is a reluctant 'chill'. So Dickens harnesses the imaginative force of an almost surreal incident to the central movement of the text, making it a matter not of action but reaction, a drama of response. With this inward movement we are taken back, like Pip: we are reminded of the 'young man' on the marshes; reminded of Miss Havisham's betrayal; alerted to the present threat both to Magwitch and to Pip himself.

As Chapter 47 closes, Pip resolves to be 'very cautious indeed'. The comic interlude intended to divert the ennui of the opening has been subverted into melodrama, but this too has shifted, back into the dynamic development of the narrative—against our expectations.

## THE COUNTERPOINT OF RELATED NARRATIVES

Anticipation, peripeteia and disappointment are consistent features of narrative structural control throughout *Great Expectations,* although our two extracts (part four and part twenty-nine) show that they may operate in both directions: to satisfy or to stimulate the reader's expectations, but always to shift towards a new accommodation. The unitary method of composition, in chapters, parts and volumes, looks simple and cumulative, but the effects are varied through an interplay of recognition and surprise. This complex construction is further enriched by the counterpoint of distinct but related narratives, as Pip's story is interrupted and supported by what we learn of those around him.

These interpolations contribute structurally as well as thematically to the novel, since we meet and accommodate them with those very responses of surprise and recognition which distinguish our reading of Pip's story. They come, of course, in sequence—the fundamental structure of all texts—but we can consider them also, as we do in reading, according to theme, mode, or tone. So we find a series of stories about the neglected child, for example, which contextualise Pip's central fable; each one is different, not just in the main character, but in presentation. Joe's history (Chapter 7) and Magwitch's (Chapter 42) both start with a suffering child, but they take divergent lines, since Joe's is the story of patience and goodness while Magwitch moves through crime towards his death in jail. Good and bad, however, are held together (despite the distance that separates them in the text) by certain features of narration. Both are told in the first person, and both are told to Pip (though on the second occasion Herbert is present too). While the content is different, the style is rather similar, marked by short declarative sentences, repetition as a device of emphasis and coherence, and a curiously dispassionate, almost comical, sense of irony. Thus Joe's introductory summary:

> I'll tell you. My father, Pip, he were given to drink, and when he were overtook with drink, he hammered away at my mother, most onmerciful. It were a'most the only hammering he did, indeed, 'xcepting at myself. And he hammered at me with a wigour only to be equalled by the wigour with which he didn't hammer at his anwil.—You're a listening and understanding, Pip?

bears a close comparison with Magwitch's:

> I am not a going fur to tell you my life, like a song or a story-book. But to give it you short and handy, I'll put it at once into a mouthful of English. In jail and out of jail, in jail and out of jail. There you've got it. That's *my* life pretty much, down to such times as I got shipped off, arter Pip stood my friend.
>
> I've been done everything to, pretty well—except hanged. I've been locked up, as much as a silver tea-kettle. I've been carted here and carted there, and put out of this town and put out of that town, and stuck in the stocks, and whipped and worried and drove. I've no more notion where I was born, than you have—if so much. I first become aware of myself down in Essex, a thieving turnips for my living. Summun had

run away from me—a man—a tinker—and he'd took the fire with him, and left me wery cold.

The similarities between Joe's tale and Magwitch's help to indicate how they offer two alternative models for the development of Pip's own story. And both Joe and Magwitch, having suffered through their own fathers, act as foster parents to the orphaned child. Which will exercise the determining influence on him? Pip rejects each one in turn, but then comes to accept and love both. The complexities of their relationships, and the subtleties of these narrative echoes and distinctions, come eventually to illuminate the contradictory and painful tendencies within Pip's own character, which his fortunes both shape and reflect.

# Repetition in
# *Great Expectations*

Douglas Brooks-Davies

Douglas Brooks-Davies analyzes Dickens's use of
repetition in *Great Expectations* to unify the story
both in the original serial publication and in the first
three-volume version of the novel. In the original serial version, thematic repetitions tie one week's installment to the next. In the three-volume version, each
volume corresponds to a stage in Pip's life. Brooks-
Davies notes that a pattern of similar lines recurs at
the end of the first and third stages, creating an echo
quality and a unifying effect. Douglas Brooks-Davies
has taught English at the University of Leeds and
the University of Manchester in England. He is the
author of several books, among them *Number and
Pattern in the Eighteenth-Century Novel* and *Fielding,
Dickens, Gosse, Iris Murdoch and Oedipal "Hamlet."*

*Great Expectations* begins in a churchyard and returns to that
same churchyard in the final chapter with Pip placing the
image of his young self in the form of Joe's and Biddy's son
Pip—'I again!'—'on a certain tombstone' from which he points
to the parental graves on which Pip the elder had meditated
so hard in chapter 1 (a comparison with Dickens's encounter
with himself as 'the very queer small boy' is inevitable).

The novel's structure is thus circular: a fact readily apparent to us as readers of a modern one-volume text, as also to
readers of the three-volume edition of October 1861, but one
that the weekly serialization of *Great Expectations* in Dickens's recently founded periodical *All the Year Round* from 1
December 1860 to 3 August 1861 concealed. Its weekly readers, whatever Dickens's overall plan for the novel's plot, encountered a growing and developing story. They could write
to its author and hope to change or influence the narrative.

Excerpted from *Charles Dickens:* Great Expectations by Douglas Brooks-Davies. Copyright ©1989 by Douglas Brooks-Davies. Reprinted by permission of Penguin Books Ltd.

They could affect authorial strategies by doing the most dreaded thing of all, withholding their money; for when sales fall off a serial novelist knows that he is failing his public. For the weekly readers, therefore, Dickens devised smaller-scale structures, often based on the best-seller technique of mystification. One of *Great Expectations*'s early reviewers, Edwin Whipple, commented on how successful Dickens had been in this respect when he wrote that he had read this novel

> as we have read all Mr Dickens's previous works, as it appeared in instalments, and can testify to the felicity with which expectation was excited and prolonged, and to the series of surprises which accompanied the unfolding of the plot of the story. *(Atlantic Monthly,* September 1861)

## THEMATIC REPETITIONS IN THE SERIAL VERSION

As well as suspense, surprise and mystification, however, Dickens developed a technique of *thematic repetitions* between the endings of the weekly parts. Normally a serial episode comprised a two-chapter module; but that depended on the length of the chapters involved, and so occasionally an instalment consisted of one long chapter, as in the cases of chapters 5 and 8. The Penguin edition marks the end of each instalment with an asterisk, thereby making it easy to see, for instance, how the conclusion of instalment 1's stolen pie and file and Pip's stealthy escape from the house on to the marshes (end of chapter 2) are relived in the ending of instalment 2 (end of chapter 4) with the pork pie's loss about to be discovered and Pip fleeing in terror only to run 'head foremost' at the house door into a group of soldiers, one of whom offers him a pair of handcuffs.

The handcuffs suggest Pip's feeling of guilt over the theft and mark his acquisition of an equivalent of Magwitch's leg-irons, which are the reason he stole the file in the first place. The means of liberating Magwitch (the file) thus symbolically binds Pip to him, as the soldiers announce by bringing the handcuffs and then (opening sentence of chapter 5, beginning of instalment 3), by a pun which opens up vistas of surreality, turning into a file themselves: 'The apparition of a file of soldiers . . .'.

Another metamorphosis of the handcuffs occurs at the close of instalment 3 (end of chapter 5) where the logic of repetitive structuring turns them into the 'massive rusty chains' of the prison ship which no file can saw through. But note that the file, Joe's file, is reintroduced by the stranger in chapter 10 and 'haunts' Pip at chapter 10's close: 'I was haunted by the file too. A dread possessed me that . . . [it] would reappear . . . in my sleep I saw the file coming at me out of a door'. (The end of chapter 10 also marks the end of instalment 6.)

Meanwhile, at the end of chapter 5 and of instalment 3, Magwitch relieves Pip of guilt over the pie by saying that he stole it himself, thus once more answering the end of instalment 1.

Again at the end of instalment 3, as the two convicts are received into the prison ship 'the ends of the torches were flung hissing into the water, and went out, as if it were all over with [Magwitch]'. This is an image of Magwitch's death and of Pip's and society's willingness to erase all memory of him. As such it anticipates the end of instalment 4 (last paragraph of chapter 7) when it is again night and Pip leaves Joe for the first time and the stars—themselves symbolic anticipations of chilly and remote Estella ('the star') in the next instalment (chapter 8)—twinkle but 'without throwing any light on' Pip's various mental queries about the visit to Miss Havisham he is just setting out on. The extinguished torches 'become' non-illumining stars by the same structural and imaginative logic that turned the file into the ghostly apparition of a row of soldiers and the handcuffs into massive rusty mooring chains. And the equation of torches with stars makes Pip's journey to Estella a farewell to Joe that parallels the relegation of Magwitch to the deathly blackness of the Hulks: Magwitch and Joe merge symbolically as Pip begins his progress to gentility.

## THE SIGNIFICANCE OF REPETITION

The Penguin text's asterisks enable any reader to pursue the kind of enquiry I have begun here. What the parallels and metamorphoses of one image into another reveal in the end, though, is that repetition is fundamental to the meaning of the narrative. The repetitions tell us that Pip's narrative is actually *about* repetition; that it is about a man whose imaginative life is dominated by a small number of obsessive images and concerns, most, if not all, of which derive from his preoccupation with himself as an orphan. This preoccupation turns him into a man who insistently recreates images of parents and the loss of parents in almost every direction he turns.

Repetition even undermines the sense of movement fostered by Pip's journey to London to establish himself as a gentleman. Not only is the end of that journey marked by Magwitch's return as Pip's 'second father' (chapter 39); its beginning in chapters 20 and 21 confronts Pip with two plaster death-masks in Jaggers's office that are somewhat reminiscent in their twoness and criminality of the two convicts who struggled in the ditch in chapter 5. It also confronts him, in Barnard's Inn, the site of his first London lodgings, with a grisly cemetery of a wasteland that combines chapter 1's churchyard with the overgrown wilderness of Satis House. Barnard's Inn turns out in addition to be inhabited by Herbert Pocket, the 'pale young gentleman' of Satis House (chapter 11).

### STAGES IN THE THREE-VOLUME VERSION

If it is a fact that in these and other details Dickens's serial (the noun was, according to the *Oxford English Dictionary,* first used with reference to a Dickens novel) proceeds not so much serially as through repetitive echoes, instalments that have as their goal the Magwitch and churchyard of the beginning, it is nevertheless also a fact that the book version, particularly in its three-volume form, contributes to the illusion that Pip actually progresses, and that he does so in three distinct *stages,* one for each of the three volumes of the original publication in book format: volume 1, chapters 1–19, at the end of which we reach the conclusion of 'the first stage of Pip's expectations'; volume 2, chapters 20–39, at the end of which we have reached 'the end of the second stage of Pip's expectations'; and volume 3, chapters 40–59, at the end of which we are, perhaps significantly, told nothing at all.

The word *stage* is wonderfully ambiguous, exactly right for Pip's journey that is really no journey. It suggests three things: the *sections of a journey* as undertaken by a stagecoach (but in this connection *stage* was often used to refer not so much to the journey as to the stopping places that divided the journey into its several stages); the *site of a dramatic presentation* (that platform within the circumscribed limits of which players act out their roles); and the *gallows* (*stage* as 'a scaffold for execution', as the *Oxford English Dictionary* defines it).

Does Dickens mean us to infer these three levels of meaning from Pip's narrative, gathering as we do so that it is about a journey by stops rather than starts involving the acting out of a part that is fixated on death, and especially death by hanging? I am sure that he does. Consider the pirate hanged from the gibbet (end of chapter 1), Miss Havisham 'hanging ... by the neck' (end of chapter 8), and Magwitch's conviction that he 'should of a certainty be hanged if took' at the end of chapter 39, just at the conclusion of 'the second *stage* of Pip's expectations'. Then consider the way play-acting is used as a theme in the novel to underline the hollowness of Pip's gentility. Each stage of the novel, in fact, sees Pip either acting or learning to act, from the moment when he wonders why he 'was going to play at Miss Havisham's, and what on earth [he] was expected to play at' (chapter 7) and Miss Havisham utters her teasingly ambiguous, 'I have a sick fancy that I want to see some play' (chapter 8).

Moreover, each of the three stages finds Pip shadowed by the figure of Wopsle, whose increasing failure to take the London stage by storm comments on Pip's own failure as an actor in the drama of urbane gentility. More precisely than that, in each stage Wopsle performs before Pip a play which relates in a more or less obvious way to Pip's situation, functioning like one of those microcosmic mirrors in a Van Eyck painting, or like *Hamlet*'s play within the play. The first of these is the eighteenth-century playwright George Lillo's *The London Merchant; or, the History of George Barnwell* (1731), still popular on the nineteenth-century stage, a reading of which Wopsle compels Pip to attend in chapter 15; the second is *Hamlet* itself (chapter 31, but attended and described by Joe earlier, in chapter 27); the third is an unnamed play with accompanying pantomime in chapter 47.

### LINES THAT ECHO

Finally, just as the instalment endings sustain a repetitively chiming dialogue with each other in the manner noted above, so do the final paragraphs of each of the three stages have an echoic relationship.

At the end of stage 1 'the mists had all solemnly risen now, and the world lay spread before' Pip as he rides on his way to London (chapter 19); at the end of stage 3 in its published form, Pip takes Estella's hand 'and, as the morning mists had risen long ago when I first left the forge, so, the evening mists were rising now' (chapter 59); while at the end of stage 2, in contrast, after Magwitch's return (chapter 39) 'the clocks of the Eastward churches were striking five, the candles were wasted out, the fire was dead, and the wind and rain intensified the thick black darkness'.

Two paragraphs concluding with rising mists frame a paragraph that ends in darkness. Rising mists suggest optimism, however unjustified it may turn out to be; thick rain and misty blackness are images of the deepest despair.

What is perhaps less immediately obvious is the way each of these stage endings is rooted in the last lines of Milton's *Paradise Lost,* the moment when Adam and Eve are finally expelled from Eden after the Fall:

> They looking back, all the eastern side beheld
> Of Paradise, so late their happy seat,
> Waved over by that flaming brand, the gate
> With dreadful faces thronged and fiery arms:
> Some natural tears they dropped, but wiped them soon;
> The world was all before them, where to choose
> Their place of rest, and providence their guide:
> They hand in hand with wandering steps and slow,
> Through Eden took their solitary way.
>
> (Book 12, lines 641–9)

Pip's 'the world lay spread before me' is clearly Miltonic (line 646 of the above passage) rather than a reminiscence of Wordsworth's recollection of the line at the opening of *The Prelude,* Book 1 as he revisits the maternal landscape of his childhood ('escaped/From the vast city, where I long had pined/A discontented sojourner: now free,/... The earth is all before me').

What the Miltonic echo tells us (for it works as an *allusion* rather than as an incidental or coincidental borrowing) is that *Great Expectations,* like *Paradise Lost,* is a narrative about loss—primal loss—and about a subsequent existence devoted to ways of coping with that loss. Milton's poem is built on the Christian myth and the idea of paradise restored through the second Adam, Christ. *Great Expectations,* despite the appearance of Christian symbolism in it, is psychologically rather than theologically oriented. It confronts us and it leaves us with a solitary Pip who is still the victim of the parental loss that he understood to be fundamental to his character and perceptions of things in the churchyard on that Christmas Eve all those years ago in chapter 1. There is no Saviour for Pip. The world that lies spread before *him* turns out to be filthy with London grime and decay, haunted by Magwitch and by Pip's obsessive returns to Satis with its buried old woman and her adopted daughter.

It is possible, I think, to argue that *Paradise Lost* has an even more precise significance than this for Dickens's novel. For Wordsworth, in *The Prelude*, childhood is equated with imaginative and personal liberty. If he can return to childhood (literally by visiting the landscape of his boyhood, imaginatively by remembering and writing about it), his Eden is recaptured. In *Great Expectations* however, Dickens produces for Pip a spread-out world that is repetitively inscribed with reminders of the loss of his parents: deathmasks, Barnard's Inn as burial ground, and so on. How does this relate to *Paradise Lost*? By suggesting that Pip's desolate world, built as it is on the loss of father and mother, is somehow a fallen world minus its Adam and Eve. Horrified at their absence, Pip has to reinvent them. Magwitch is thus brought into being as a fallen Adam inhabiting a marshy wilderness; and Miss Havisham is Pip's fascinated resurrection of Mother Eve, dwelling within the even more desolate wilderness of Satis House and its grounds.

Pip's attempt to link with Estella is therefore, on this level, an attempt to duplicate the marriage between his own parents perceived as an image of Edenic happiness. That much the published ending of the novel tells us with its echo of the ending of stage 1 (the rising mists) and its holding of hands ('I took her hand in mine, and we went out of the ruined place'; compare Adam and Eve 'hand in hand'). But for Pip, it can only be an image, can only be imagined, not achieved. Pip never overcomes the loss of his parents sufficiently to have a life of his own. He is always an exile without a mate because he is haunted by his parents as a lost, disowned, and dead Adam and Eve.

# Chronology

**1812**

Charles Dickens born February 7, to John and Elizabeth Dickens; War of 1812 begins with United States.

**1814**

John Dickens transferred to London.

**1817**

John Dickens transferred to Chatham.

**1821**

Charles Dickens starts school.

**1822**

John Dickens transferred to London.

**1824**

John Dickens arrested for debt and sent to Marshalsea Prison; Charles Dickens begins work at Warren's Blacking Factory.

**1824–1826**

Attends Wellington House Academy in London.

**1827**

Works as law clerk; improves his education at the British Museum Reading Room.

**1830**

Meets Maria Beadnell.

**1831**

Becomes reporter for the *Mirror of Parliament.*

**1832**

Becomes staff writer for the *True Sun.*

**1833**

First published piece appears in the *Monthly Magazine*; slavery abolished in British Empire.

**1834**

Becomes staff writer on the *Morning Chronicle;* street sketches published in the *Evening Chronicle;* meets Catherine Hogarth.

**1836**

*Sketches by Boz* published in book form; marries Catherine Hogarth; plays *The Strange Gentleman* and *The Village Coquettes* produced at St. James's Theater; meets John Forster, a lifelong friend and biographer; Ralph Waldo Emerson publishes *Nature.*

**1836–1837**

*Pickwick Papers* published in monthly installments.

**1837**

*Pickwick Papers* published in book form; begins installments of *Oliver Twist* in *Bentley's Miscellany;* play *Is She Your Wife?* produced at St. James's Theater; first child, Charles, born; Catherine's sister Mary Hogarth dies suddenly; Victoria becomes queen of England; Thomas Carlyle publishes *The French Revolution.*

**1838**

*Nicholas Nickleby* appears in installments; *Oliver Twist* published in book form; first daughter, Mary, born; first railroad train enters London.

**1839**

*Nicholas Nickleby* published in book form; second daughter, Kate, born; People's Charter, stating six demands for voting and representation for the poor; Chinese-British Opium Wars begin; end 1860.

**1840**

Dickens edits *Master Humphrey's Clock*, a weekly; *The Old Curiosity Shop* appears in installments and in book form; England annexes New Zealand; Queen Victoria marries Prince Albert; James Fenimore Cooper publishes *The Pathfinder.*

**1841**

*Barnaby Rudge* appears in *Master Humphrey's Clock* and in book form; Dickens's second son, Walter, born; the magazine *Punch* founded; Ralph Waldo Emerson publishes *Essays.*

**1842**

Dickens tours America with Catherine; *American Notes* published; Alfred, Lord Tennyson publishes *Poems*; anesthesia first used in surgery.

## 1843

*Martin Chuzzlewit* appears in monthly installments; "A Christmas Carol" published for Christmas; William Wordsworth becomes poet laureate.

## 1844

Dickens tours Italy and Switzerland; *Martin Chuzzlewit* published in book form; "The Chimes" published for Christmas; Dickens's third son, Francis, born; first message by Morse's telegraph.

## 1845

Dickens produces the play *Every Man in His Humour;* "The Cricket on the Hearth" published for Christmas; Dickens's fourth son, Alfred, born; Edgar Allan Poe publishes *The Raven and Other Poems.*

## 1846

Dickens creates and edits the *Daily News; Dombey and Son* appears in monthly installments; *Pictures from Italy* published in book form; "The Battle of Life: A Love Story" published for Christmas; Irish potato famine results in mass emigration to United States; repeal of Corn Laws, which regulated grain trade and restricted imports; Elias Howe invents sewing machine.

## 1847

Dickens starts a theatrical company and takes *Every Man in His Humour* on a benefit tour; Dickens's fifth son, Sydney, born; Charlotte Brontë publishes *Jane Eyre;* Emily Bronte publishes *Wuthering Heights;* Henry Wadsworth Longfellow publishes *Evangeline.*

## 1848

Theatrical company performs for Queen Victoria; theatrical company performs *The Merry Wives of Windsor* to raise money for preservation of Shakespeare's birthplace; *Dombey and Son* published in book form; "The Haunted Man" published for Christmas; Dickens's sister Fanny dies.

## 1849

*David Copperfield* appears in monthly installments; Dickens's sixth son, Henry, born; Henry David Thoreau publishes "Civil Disobedience."

## 1850

*David Copperfield* published in book form; Dickens establishes and edits *Household Words;* Dickens's third daughter,

Dora Annie, born, dies in infancy; Elizabeth Barrett Browning publishes *Sonnets from the Portuguese;* Tennyson becomes poet laureate; Nathaniel Hawthorne publishes *The Scarlet Letter.*

## 1851

Dickens and theatrical company perform charity plays; Dickens's father, John, dies; Nathaniel Hawthorne publishes *The House of the Seven Gables;* Herman Melville publishes *Moby-Dick.*

## 1852

*Bleak House* appears in monthly installments; *A Child's History of England* published in book form; Dickens's seventh son, Edward, born; Harriet Beecher Stowe publishes *Uncle Tom's Cabin.*

## 1853

*Bleak House* published in book form; Dickens gives first public reading from the Christmas books; travels to France and Italy.

## 1854

*Hard Times* appears in installments in *Household Words;* *Hard Times* published in book form; Henry David Thoreau publishes *Walden;* Crimean War begins; ends 1856.

## 1855

*Little Dorrit* appears in monthly installments; Dickens and family travel to Paris; Walt Whitman publishes *Leaves of Grass.*

## 1856

Dickens purchases Gad's Hill.

## 1857

*Little Dorrit* published in book form; Dickens spends year on theatrical productions.

## 1858

Dickens separates from Catherine; Dickens gives public readings; Henry Wadsworth Longfellow publishes *The Courtship of Miles Standish.*

## 1859

Dickens ends *Household Words;* begins *All the Year Round;* *A Tale of Two Cities* appears in *All the Year Round* and in book form.

**1860**

*Great Expectations* appears in weekly installments.

**1861**

*Great Expectations* published in book form; *The Uncommercial Traveller,* a collection, published; George Eliot publishes *Silas Marner;* U.S. Civil War begins; ends 1865.

**1862**

Dickens gives many public readings; travels to Paris; Victor Hugo publishes *Les Misérables;* Lincoln issues Emancipation Proclamation, freeing slaves.

**1863**

Dickens gives public readings in London and Paris; mother, Elizabeth, dies; Lincoln delivers Gettysburg Address.

**1864**

*Our Mutual Friend* appears in monthly installments.

**1865**

Dickens suffers a stroke, leaving him lame; *Our Mutual Friend* published in book form; *The Uncommercial Traveller,* a second collection, published; Lewis Carroll publishes *Alice in Wonderland;* Leo Tolstoy publishes *War and Peace;* rapid postwar industrialization in United States.

**1866**

Dickens gives public readings in Scotland and Ireland; Fyodor Dostoyevsky publishes *Crime and Punishment.*

**1867**

Dickens travels to America to give public readings; England grants dominion status for Canada.

**1868**

Dickens gives public readings in England; Louisa May Alcott publishes *Little Women.*

**1869**

Dickens begins *The Mystery of Edwin Drood;* Mark Twain publishes *Innocents Abroad;* imprisonment for debt abolished; Suez Canal opened.

**1870**

Dickens gives farewell public reading in London; *The Mystery of Edwin Drood* appears in monthly installments; becomes seriously ill, June 8; dies, June 9; buried in Poet's Corner, Westminster Abbey, June 14.

# FOR FURTHER RESEARCH

## ABOUT CHARLES DICKENS AND HIS WORKS

Walter Allen, *The English Novel: A Short Critical History.* New York: E.P. Dutton, 1955.

François Basch, *Relative Creatures: Victorian Women in Society and the Novel.* New York: Schocken Books, 1974.

Mary Lamberton Becker, *Introducing Charles Dickens.* New York: Dodd, Mead, 1940.

David Cecil, *Victorian Novelists.* Chicago: University of Chicago Press, 1938.

G.K. Chesterton, *Charles Dickens: The Last of the Great Men.* New York: The Readers Club, 1942.

Richard Church, *The Growth of the English Novel.* New York: Barnes and Noble, 1961.

Robert Alan Donovan, *The Shaping Vision: Imagination in the English Novel from Defoe to Dickens.* Ithaca, NY: Cornell University Press, 1966.

Wolf Mankowitz, *Dickens of London.* New York: Macmillan, 1976.

Jo Murtry, *Victorian Life and Victorian Fiction: A Companion for the American Reader.* Hamden, CT: Archon Books, 1979.

S. Diana Neill, *A Short History of the English Novel.* London: Jarrolds Publishers, 1951.

Harland S. Nelson, *Charles Dickens.* Boston: Twayne, 1981.

William Lyon Phelps, *The Advance of the English Novel.* New York: Dodd, Mead, 1916.

J.B. Priestley, *Charles Dickens and His World.* New York: Charles Scribner's Sons, 1961.

Barry V. Qualls, *The Secular Pilgrims of Victorian Fiction:*

*The Novel Book of Life.* Cambridge, England: Cambridge University Press, 1982.

Dorothy Van Ghent, *The English Novel: Form and Function.* New York: Rinehart, 1953.

Merryn Williams, *Women in the English Novel, 1800–1900.* New York: St. Martin's Press, 1984.

Angus Wilson, *The World of Charles Dickens.* London: Martin Secker & Warburg, 1970.

## ABOUT DICKENS'S TIMES

James Truslow Adams, *Empire on the Seven Seas: The British Empire 1784–1939.* New York: Charles Scribner's Sons, 1940.

Arthur Bryant, *Pageant of England 1840–1940.* New York: Harper and Brothers, 1941.

——, *Spirit of England.* London: William Collins Sons, 1982.

C.E. Carrington and J. Hampden Jackson, *A History of England.* Cambridge, England: Cambridge University Press, 1945.

John W. Derry, *A Short History of Nineteenth-Century England.* London: Blandford Press, 1963.

Margaret Drabble, *For Queen and Country: Britain in the Victorian Age.* New York: Seabury Press, 1979.

Carlton J.H. Hayes and Margareta Faissler, *Modern Times: The French Revolution to the Present.* New York: Macmillan, 1966.

Marjorie Quennell and C.H.B. Quennell, *A History of Everyday Things in England: The Rise of Industrialism 1733–1851.* London: B.T. Batsford, 1933.

——, *A History of Everyday Things in England 1851–1914.* London: B.T. Batsford, 1934.

Philip A.M. Taylor, ed., *The Industrial Revolution in Britain: Triumph or Disaster?* Lexington, MA: D.C. Heath, 1970.

G.M. Trevelyan, *History of England.* Vol 3. Garden City, NY: Doubleday, Anchor Books, 1926.

R.J. White, *The Horizon Concise History of England.* New York: American Heritage, 1971.

**ORGANIZATIONS TO CONTACT**

Dickens Society (DS)
Department of Humanities and Arts
Worcester Polytechnic Institute
Worcester, MA 01609-2280

Phone: (508) 831-5572
Fax: (508) 831-5878

The society conducts and supports research and general interest in the life, times, and works of Dickens. Its scholarly journal, the *Dickens Quarterly*, includes an annual index and bibliographies.

# WORKS BY CHARLES DICKENS

"A Dinner at Poplar Walk," in *Monthly Magazine* (1833)

"Street Sketches," in *Evening Chronicle* (1834)

*Sketches by Boz* (1836)

*The Strange Gentleman*, a play (1836)

*The Village Coquettes*, a play (1836)

*Pickwick Papers* (1837)

*Is She Your Wife?* a play (1837)

*Oliver Twist* (1839)

*Nicholas Nickleby* (1839)

*The Old Curiosity Shop* (1840)

*Barnaby Rudge* (1841)

*American Notes* (1842)

"A Christmas Carol" (1843)

*Martin Chuzzlewit* (1844)

"The Chimes" (1844)

"A Cricket on the Hearth" (1845)

*Pictures from Italy* (1846)

"The Battle of Life: A Love Story" (1846)

"The Haunted Man" (1848)

*Dombey and Son* (1848)

*David Copperfield* (1850)

*A Child's History of England* (1852)

*Bleak House* (1853)

*Hard Times* (1854)

*Little Dorrit* (1857)

*A Tale of Two Cities* (1859)

*Great Expectations* (1861)

*The Uncommercial Traveller* (1861)

*Our Mutual Friend* (1865)

*The Uncommercial Traveller*, second edition (1865)

*The Mystery of Edwin Drood* (published posthumously)

# INDEX